Praise for
Innovate with iPad

"In this thoughtful book, Kristen and Karen, two masterful educators, provide practical and approachable ideas for using open-ended tools to help students demonstrate understanding and reveal their learning processes. This is an invaluable resource for anyone teaching students in early elementary school with any kind of technology access. The ideas shared in this book unlock the power of technology to transfer agency to learners, meet them where they are, and lead them where they need to be."

—**Dr. Reshan Richards**, co-Author, *Blending Leadership*, Department of Math, Science & Technology, Teachers College, Columbia University, Chief Learning Officer and co-Founder, Explain Everything

"In *Innovate with iPad: Lessons to Transform Learning*, Karen Lirenman and Kristen Wideen have designed a comprehensive selection of clearly laid out numeracy, literacy, science, and social studies lessons. They include step-by-step instructions on how to use open-ended creative apps across these subjects in innovative ways to get students to show and express their thinking. This would be a perfect book for a teacher starting to use iPads in K-3 classrooms, and for those who want new ideas of how to use technology in creative ways to stretch students' learning."

—**Caroline Hu Flexer**, co-Founder and CEO, Duck Duck Moose

"All teachers with iPads should read this book. Your students will thank you for it!"

—**Dan Amos**, developer of Book Creator for iPad

"This book is a must-read for anyone working with grade K-3 students (or their teachers) and iPads! Presenting more than sixty formative and summative assessments, using a well-chosen, small toolbox of creation apps, the authors target the higher-order thinking skills in each lesson. They provide pedagogically sound tech projects for students to demonstrate their understanding of concepts in math, ELA, science, and social studies."

—**Kathy Schrock,** Educational Technologist, kathyschrock.net

"Karen Lirenman and Kristen Wideen have created a tremendous resource for teachers who want to use iPads in meaningful ways in their classrooms. K-3 teachers will find a plethora of ideas, examples, and step-by-step instructions based on specific curricular outcomes in mathematics, language arts, and beyond. This book will be a valuable and practical part of any primary teacher's professional library."

—**Kathy Cassidy**, Grade One Teacher and Author of *Connected From the Start*

"This book is a terrific collection of iPad activities for the primary grades teacher! Kristen and Karen have curated a list of applications and tasks that all classrooms can use to support student thinking with the iPad. This resource will provide new ideas for differentiating instruction and offering students choice across the curriculum."

—**Kristin Ziemke**, Author of *Amplify*, Teacher and Learning Innovation Specialist, Big Shoulders Fund

Lessons to Transform Learning

Karen Lirenman and Kristen Wideen

Innovate with iPad

These books are available at special discounts when purchased in quantity for use as premiums, promotions, fundraising, and educational use. For inquiries and details, contact the publisher: info@mywritersconnection.com.

Published by My Writers' Connection Publishing

Library of Congress Number: On file

Paperback ISBN: 978-1-950714-06-3

eBook ISBN: 978-1-950714-07-0

CONTENTS

Foreword

iPads give students and teachers freedom from the computer in the corner of the class and bring digital learning into the messy middle of the room. Any digital device can do word processing or skill and drill practice, but the power of the iPad is how it allows us to create rich multimedia. Pictures and videos are central to using iPad, along with creation apps that transform pictures and videos into so much more. But our challenge as educators is to figure out how to move from having kids pinch, swipe, and tap on consumption apps to creating evidence of learning. *Innovate with iPad: Lessons to Transform Learning* is the book to help you move towards using iPad smoothly, creatively, and meaningfully in the classroom.

Innovate with iPad: Lessons to Transform Learning is the book you and every educator with access to iPad needs to make a fast transition to using iPad for learning. First, this book will help anyone be a smoother iPad user. This book declutters and demystifies the question about which apps to use so teachers and students can quickly become fluent on iPad. By focusing on five central apps, you'll spend less time pushing buttons and more time getting students thinking. The lessons range from using a single app to flowing several apps together for more sophisticated products of student learning. The goal is to become a smooth and skilled user and quickly get to the learning.

Next, the authors present clear lessons that use the device in creative ways. This book is for the busy teacher who needs and wants compressed but easy-to-follow ideas that can be used the next period or the next day. It can be scary opening up these creation apps because many of them are like a blank canvas waiting for the teacher and student to be the creatives. The lessons include ideas for how to get kids creating artifacts that are visually appealing and reveal student understanding. With these activities, you will get a better sense of what your students know and are able to do with less marking than on a traditional worksheet. You and your fellow educators will see how to use iPad creatively to see inside your students' hearts and minds.

Finally, this book is about making meaning together across the curriculum. The key with this book is that every lesson is loaded not only with best practices for using iPad, but also the most current and up-to-date teaching methods in math, language, and the content areas. In math, the focus is on problem solving, fluid and flexible understanding of numbers, and real-world math. In language, there is an emphasis on reading strategies and critical thinking in both fiction and nonfiction texts. In science and social studies, the activities engage students in the inquiry process. *Innovate with iPad* explores the best ways of integrating iPad with the best practices for literacy, numeracy, and inquiry learning.

The book concludes with a chapter on self-assessment. In the end, the authors highlight a movement to go beyond engaging students with flashy games and towards empowering learners with creating artifacts that students assess themselves. In every lesson, the learning goals are made clear to students and so it is fitting that learners also be given the power to judge for themselves their degree of achievement. This self-assessment brings the student into the centre of the learning with the iPad and the teacher by their side as guiding support. This book will transform the classroom by bringing teachers up to speed with smooth iPad use, creative lessons and activities for learning, and meaningful activities that are based on strong pedagogy.

The authors, Karen Lirenman and Kristen Wideen, are your support and your students' support for using iPad in the classroom. These early adopters of iPad have over five years of classroom experience with iPad and have tested and honed their best lessons for this book. These two educators live on opposite sides of the country, have different but complementary teaching styles, and different work experiences. Their seasoned and unique voices from the field combine seamlessly into one strong voice that guides us through the journey of innovating with iPad for learning. In addition to the book, these teachers share a fully loaded website with activities and Task Cards that can be used immediately in the classroom. Karen and Kristen have removed all the barriers for getting going with iPad and help fast forward every iPad teacher's journey for the benefit of our students. They are two of the best teachers I know and have both been dedicated to the best and the practical. I know you'll love reading their lessons and seeing the magic that will take place in your classroom. This book is also a model for all to follow. *Innovate with iPad: Lessons to Transform Learning* is both a practical guide and an invitation to use their ideas as a foundation and go forward to create your own smooth, creative, and meaningful iPad lessons.

—Michelle Cordy
Teacher, Applied Researcher
@cordym

Introduction

As two primary school teachers, we feel fortunate to have access to iPads in our classrooms. When we initially received our iPads, we weren't sure how to best use them, so we gravitated toward finding and downloading apps to support what we were already doing. We quickly realized, though, that having iPads in our classrooms allows for more innovative and student-centred teaching. And once we discovered a few simple, albeit powerful, open-ended creative apps, our students' learning—and our teaching—were transformed.

This book is a collection of lessons we've created to help you start your own journey teaching with iPad. While this book was originally written for classroom use, we realize it has great potential in the home learning environment as well. In fact, we feel that it is very important for children to see the iPad as a tool for learning at a young age instead of just an entertainment device. When children use their devices to create books, videos and digital artifacts, they begin to see that the iPad has multiple purposes and a huge potential to grow with them. The lessons included here are ideal for the homeschooled child, or for additional home practice. The lessons are open-ended and allow a child to really show what they know in ways that work best for them. In addition they are simple to follow, only use one or two apps, and can easily be adapted to any content area. As a mom, Kristen often uses the lessons found in this book to help support her own two children's learning. These lessons allow all learners to make their thinking visible in innovative and creative ways.

In each lesson, you'll find the "why" and "how," as well as extensions and quick tips. Many lessons also include sample images, links to real students' work, and a downloadable student Task Card. Before we jump into the lessons, here's a quick look at what you'll find in *Innovate with iPad*.

Chapter 1

We will introduce you to the five apps we use most frequently in our classrooms: Pic Collage, Popplet, Draw and Tell, Book Creator, and Explain Everything. In this chapter, we will also explain the iPad comfort levels referred to in the remainder of the book.

Chapter 2

We use iPad in numeracy lessons to explore operations and algebraic thinking, numbers and operations in base ten, measurement and data, and geometry. You can modify most of these lessons to meet your students' individual needs.

Chapter 3

These lessons focus on using iPad to support a literacy program. We explore methods for teaching reading and writing fluency, along with developing word sense.

Chapter 4

We present science lessons that support exploring living things, energy and forces, the environment, and working scientifically. Many of these lessons also support the inquiry process.

Chapter 5

We focus on social studies lessons that look at students' personal growth, health, and community.

Chapter 6

In the book's final chapter, we explore how your students can use their iPads to help take control of their learning by becoming a part of the self-assessment process.

We believe you'll find that by simply downloading a few basic, open-ended creation apps, your students will engage in the learning process and demonstrate their new-found knowledge in the way that works best for them. Whether you have access to one iPad for your entire class or one for each student, these lessons will help you transform learning in your classroom.

chapter one

Getting Started

A few years back, we were both extremely fortunate to hear that we would be given iPads to use in our classrooms. Unsure of the full potential of iPad, we ferociously downloaded drill and practice apps along with some digital book apps as a way to incorporate iPads into our environments. The children loved them because they were having so much "fun" tapping and learning. They would re-play the funny parts of the stories over and over again and rush to the iPad to beat their high scores in their favourite math apps. To the student, the iPad felt like the *best learning ever*. However, as educators, we quickly realized we could do so much more with iPad than play with a few apps. We were in the beginning stages of a transformation. In terms of the SAMR Model (substitution, augmentation, modification, redefinition), we were substituting paper and pencil in favour of an iPad. As much as iPad was a "fun" way to learn, little had changed with our practice. We had only scratched the surface of what was possible.

But our students surprised us. Billy, the student who struggled to decode words, began using the iPad to help him with his reading. He learned that he could give a word a try and if he wasn't sure if he was right or not, he could tap the word and the iPad would read it to him. Mya loved to draw her thinking. She started to use the iPad not only to draw, but also to record her voice explaining those drawings. Jimmy had a thing for making movies and started filming number stories as a way to show his understanding of math. Our students wrote digital books and made high-quality products. iPad made this all possible.

As our students began to show us what really was possible with iPad, our practice moved from relying on monotonous paper-pencil tasks to our students creating digital artifacts to show their learning in new and innovative ways. iPad became an outlet for student creativity and choice. Suddenly, the possibilities for their learning became endless. Meaningful integration of iPad in our classroom had begun, but more importantly, our teaching had changed—for the better.

Once we started meaningfully integrating the iPad into our teaching, we noticed that our students gravitated toward a few simple, creative apps, including Pic Collage, Popplet, Draw and Tell, Book Creator, and Explain Everything, to show us what they had learned. Before we dive into the lessons, we want to offer a brief overview of these commonly used apps. We hope understanding these apps' capabilities will help you think about how your students can use them, too.

Pic Collage

Pic Collage lets even your youngest learners create shareable photo collages by importing images to meet a specific learning purpose. Once they've selected their photos, students can manipulate the images' size and positioning, placing images randomly in the collage or fitting them in a layout template. Students can also add text in a variety of colours and fonts, as well as stickers from Pic Collage's image library.

Popplet

Popplet is the only mind-mapping app your students will ever need. This wonderful app allows young learners to record facts, research, generate ideas, and to document and organize their learning. Simply by touching and dragging their "popples" (bubbles filled with text, images, and/or drawings), students can easily arrange their thoughts into the form of a "popplet" (mind map). They zoom in and out (pinching) to create more or less room for their popples. And once their popplet is complete, students can export it as a JPEG to their iPad's Camera Roll so they can easily access it in other apps or share it on the web.

Draw and Tell

Draw and Tell is a simple drawing, annotating, and creating app designed for young learners. Its simple interface makes it easy for students of all ages to draw, paint, and add stickers to their work. Students can also upload images from their iPad's Camera Roll and use the app's recording feature to record themselves talking about their work. When they touch the screen as they record, a blue pointer light appears which can be used as a built in laser pointer. Additionally, if a student uses Draw and Tell's stickers in their creations, they can move the stickers around the screen while making their recording, which is especially useful for sharing mathematical thinking.

Book Creator

At its most basic level, Book Creator is a book-making app that students can use to document, create, and share ideas and work samples in all content areas. Students control everything, from their book's page size and layout to its images, videos, text, stickers, voice, and music. And, as an added bonus, students can also create comics using Book Creator's comic book layouts.

One of the app's most exciting features, though, is the ability to create and then save a project to a location off the iPad (e.g., to Dropbox or on Google Drive). This allows students to then import their project back onto either their iPad or a peer's, not only freeing up storage space, but also opening up the possibility for students to combine their books, and in turn, work with each other. And while Book Creator isn't free, the variety of ways students can use it make it worth more than the few dollars that it costs.

Explain Everything

Explain Everything is a digital, recordable whiteboard app that lets students of any age document their learning by capturing photos, creating videos, designing presentations, and making books—the applications are endless. Select the app's simple interface for your youngest learners, or the more advanced one with additional tools for your older ones, and they can begin creating, annotating, recording their thinking, and collaborating.

And once a project is done, students can upload their work to Google Drive, YouTube, and Dropbox with the tap of a finger.

The lessons in this book have been clearly labelled for beginner and advanced iPad users. The lessons that are labelled "beginner" are lessons that use one app and have simple instructions to follow. These lessons are in no way only for "beginners"; they still provide rich learning opportunities for all students. The lessons that are labelled "advanced" often use a combination of apps and may involve multiple steps to complete the task. The advanced lessons are better suited for students who are fluent with the apps being used.

Throughout the book, you will see the Task Card icon which indicates that a student task card is available for download from our website InnovatewithiPad.com. In addition, we've included the Student Work icon with lessons when a student sample is available. You'll find the password to access these items on page 12.

Sample Task Card

Composing and Decomposing Numbers Using Standard and Expanded Form

Learning Goal:

• Compare two three-digit numbers based on meanings of the hundreds, tens and ones digits, using >,= and < symbols to record the results of comparisons.

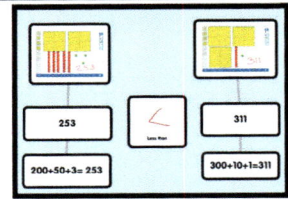

Success Criteria:
• I can build numbers up to the hundreds place with base ten blocks.
• I can compose and decompose numbers using standard and expanded form.
• I can use place value to compare the values of numbers.

I can:

Popplet

1. Open the Number Pieces app. Choose two three-digit numbers. Using the base 10 pieces, build the two numbers I chose.
2. Take a screenshot of each number built with the Number Pieces app.
3. Open the Popplet app.
4. Touch the screen to create a popple. A popple is the rectangular box that appears on the screen. Along the bottom of the popple you can chose to add text (T), draw (pen tool), or add an image (picture icon).
5. Add your two images that you created using Number Pieces.
6. Add two more popples. Write the three-digit numbers in each popple.
7. Add another 2 popples each showing the number you chose in the expanded form.
8. Add the last popple to compare the two numbers using <,=,>.

www.mrswideen.com

chapter two

Numeracy Lessons

The iPad has changed the way we teach math in our classrooms. Our students no longer do the same old worksheets; rather, they demonstrate their mathematical knowledge for us by creating personally relevant numeracy content. We've designed the following lessons to help you show your students how they can, too.

Digital Sticker Numbers

Grade Level

K–1

Subject Area

Basic Numbers

iPad Comfort Level

Beginner

Suggested Apps

Draw and Tell
Pic Collage
Doodle Buddy
Drawing Pad

Lesson Extensions

Encourage students to add their voices to their creations and count the objects to show they understand one-to-one correspondence in an app such as Draw and Tell.

Students can combine a collection of numbers and create a slideshow.

Have students choose a number smaller than five or larger than fifteen.

The Task

In this lesson, students use their app's sticker or stamp feature to represent numbers up to fifteen.

The Student's Learning Intention

• "I can build a number set up to fifteen."

The How

1. Choose a number between five and fifteen.
2. Use your app's digital stickers to represent the chosen number.
3. Label the image number.
4. Save your picture to the iPad's Camera Roll.
5. Repeat the process for other numbers, as necessary.

The Task

To really understand a number, students need to understand its value in relation to other numbers. In this activity, students choose a base number and then create a graphic that shows numbers bigger and smaller than it.

The Student's Learning Intention

- "I can show a number in relation to other numbers."
- "I can make a number one larger and one smaller."
- "I can make a number two larger and two smaller."
- "I can make a number five larger and five smaller."
- "I can make a number ten larger and ten smaller."

The How

1. Select a number.
2. Open Popplet.
3. In the centre, create the first popple and put your base number in it.
4. Create popples to the left that show the value of one less, two less, five less, and ten less.
5. Create popples to the right that show the value of one more, two more, five more, and ten more.
6. Save your popplet to the Camera Roll.

Grade Level

1–3

Subject Area

Numbers

iPad Comfort Level

Beginner

Suggested App

Popplet

Lesson Extension

Have students create popples that show multiplication facts. For example, students could multiply their base number by three or five.

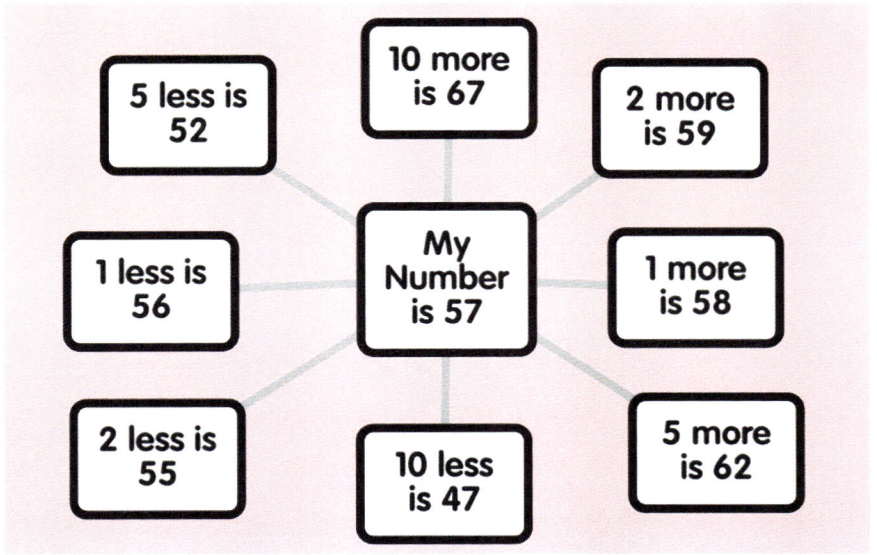

Patterning with iPad Stickers

Grade Level
PreK–3

Subject Area
Patterning

iPad Comfort Level
Advanced

Suggested App
Draw and Tell

Quick Tip
Caution students against placing stickers too close to the record button at the top because their recording may stop when they touch the stickers.

Lesson Extension
Students can create more than one pattern and explore repeating patterns with more than one attribute. Encourage your class to create growing and shrinking patterns, with repeating patterns within those patterns.

Task Card
innovatewithipad.com

Use the password **contentcreation** to access Task Cards and Student Work examples.

The Task
For this lesson, students will create a pattern with stickers and then record themselves talking about it.

The Student's Learning Intentions
- "I can create a repeating pattern."
- "I can create a repeating pattern using two or more attributes."
- "I can create a growing pattern."
- "I can create a shrinking pattern."
- "I can create a pattern that grows and shrinks."

The How
1. Open Draw and Tell.
2. Select a paper.
3. Create a pattern with stickers (right side) that reflects your learning level.
4. Use the pencil tool and label your pattern (if required).
5. Tap the microphone button to activate the mic and record yourself talking about your pattern. If you touch a sticker while recording, the sticker will move, and if you touch the screen, a blue dot will appear.
6. When you are finished recording, tap the left arrow (top left).
7. Save your creation to the iPad's Camera Roll.

Innovate with iPad

The Task

This lesson lets your students create their own addition and subtraction number stories using Draw and Tell's sticker feature.

The Student's Learning Intentions

- "I can create an addition number story."
- "I can create a subtraction number story."

The How

1. Select a number for your number story.
2. Open Draw and Tell.
3. Select a paper.
4. Draw a basic scene that can work with either an addition or subtraction story. (Drawing tools are on the right.)
5. Choose the stickers (right) that best work with the scene.
6. Write your story's number sentence.
7. Tap the microphone button to activate the mic and record your number story. While you are recording, move the stickers around to match the story. You can also touch the screen as you record; a blue dot will appear, and that helps those watching the video know what part of the screen you are talking about.
8. When you are finished, tap the left arrow (top left) to save your creation to the Camera Roll.

Grade Level

K–1

Subject Area

Addition/Subtraction

iPad Comfort Level

Beginner

Suggested App

Draw and Tell

Quick Tips

Remind your students that the iPad's built-in microphone is at the top of their iPad, and although it's very small, it is quite powerful. Direct them to speak directly into the microphone to help block out background sounds. You may also consider using an external microphone, such as a built-in mic on a headset.

Lesson Extension

Students can also use Draw and Tell to tell a non-digital number story they've created with hands-on manipulatives.

Ways to Make Ten (1)

Grade Level

K–1

Subject Area

Number Sense

iPad Comfort Level

Beginner

Suggested App

Pic Collage

Lesson Extension

You can also do this lesson with digital math manipulatives found in apps like Number Pieces and with different number values.

The Task

In this lesson, students create a collage to capture and document different ways to make ten using non-digital math manipulatives.

The Student's Learning Intention

- "I can create a collage that shows the different ways I can make ten."

The How

1. Make ten using non-digital math manipulatives, such as Cuisenaire rods, base ten units, or multi-link cubes.

2. Take a photo of each combination.

3. Repeat the first and second steps until you have at least six different ways to make ten.

4. Open Pic Collage and tap "+" to create a new collage.

5. Tap the "+" (bottom) and select a maximum of twelve photos from your Camera Roll.

6. Tap the checkmark (top right corner of the photos) to add the photos to your collage.

7. At this point, you can either organize your images freehand or tap the grid square (bottom left) and select the grid that best fits your images.

8. Tap the "+" button again, but this time, select text. Add number sentences to go with the different ways to make ten.

9. Once you have finished labelling your project, add your name to it.

10. To save your image to your iPad's Camera Roll, tap the box with the arrow pointing out from it. If you want share your image on social media, via email, or to your Google Drive, select the appropriate option.

Ways to Make Ten (2)

Grade Level
K–1

Subject Area
Number Sense

iPad Comfort Level
Beginner

Suggested App
Hands on Math Hundreds Chart (by Ventura)

Lesson Extensions

Have students import their screenshots into an app with a voice-recording feature like Draw and Tell or Explain Everything and then talk about the different ways they made ten.

Have students annotate their work with the correlating number sentences by importing their screenshots into another app like Draw and Tell.

Challenge students to use three colours for each line, encouraging them to create additional ways to make ten.

The Task

This open-ended lesson encourages students to discover different ways to make ten by playing with a hundreds chart.

The Student's Learning Intention

• "I can show different ways to make ten."

The How

1. Open the Hands on Math Hundreds Chart app by Ventura.
2. Ask yourself, "How many different ways can I cover a line of ten on a hundreds chart to represent ten?"
3. Tap the green arrow to access the hundreds chart.
4. Select the translucent square (bottom left).
5. Pick a colour and cover some of the squares in the line with numbers one through ten.
6. Choose a second colour and cover the remaining squares in the line with one through ten.
7. Repeat the process for each line, ensuring no two lines are the same.
8. Take a screenshot of your creation.

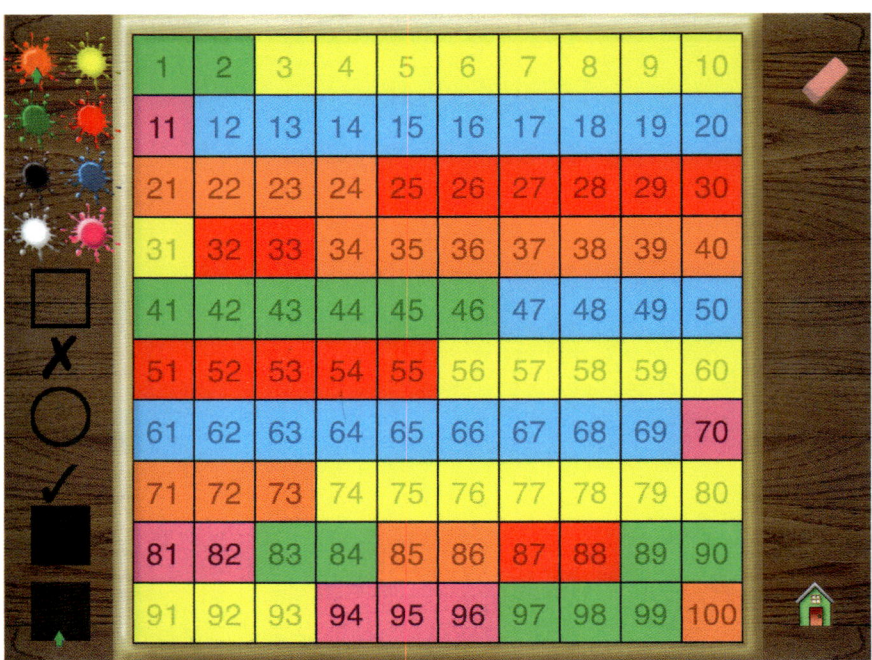

Ways to Make a Number: Part and Part-Whole Relationships

The Task

In this activity, students break down a number into different combinations of units and rods to illustrate the part and part-whole relationships numbers have. To complete this activity, students need to understand that one number can be made up of different parts.

The Student's Learning Intentions

- "I can break a number into its parts."
- "I can show more than one way to break a number into its parts."

The How

1. Select a number.
2. Open Number Pieces.
3. Using the pencil, divide your screen into four equal sections.
4. In the first section, create your number using units, rods, and flats.
5. Repeat the process in the second, third, and fourth sections using different combinations of units, rods, and flats.
6. Take a screenshot of your work and save it to the Camera Roll.

Grade Level

1–3

Subject Area

Part and Part-Whole

iPad Comfort Level

Beginner

Suggested App

Number Pieces[1]

Lesson Extension

Take this lesson a step further and have students record an explanation of their work.

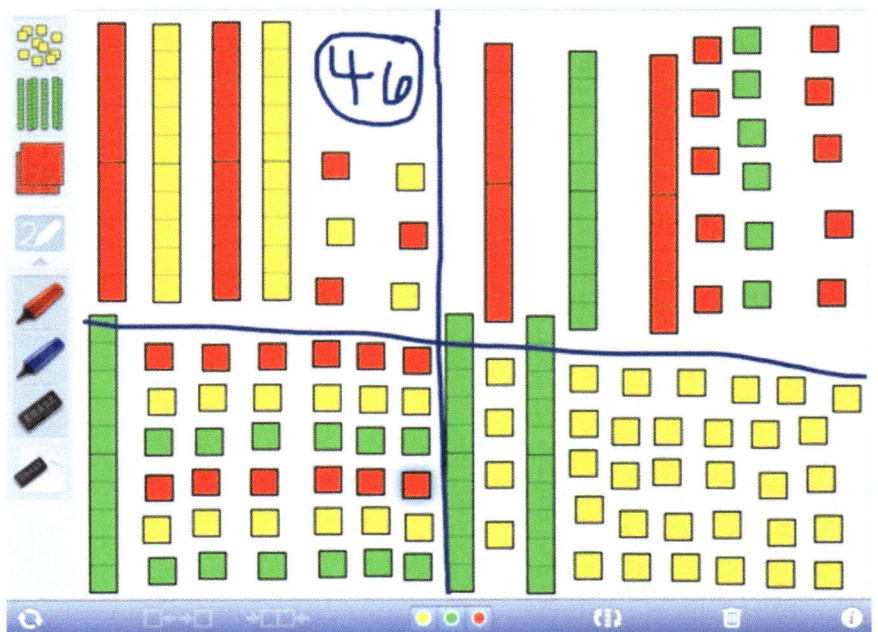

---

1 **Number Pieces is a wonderful app to use when students are exploring how to compose and decompose numbers using base ten blocks.**

One Is a Snail, Ten Is a Crab

Grade Level
K–3

Subject Area
Addition or Multiplication

iPad Comfort Level
Advanced

Suggested Apps
Drawing Pad
Draw and Tell
Doodle Buddy
**Drawing App of
Your Choice**

Lesson Extension
There are many different combinations of legs to represent every number. Encourage your students to create multiple answers to the question, and then have them add their answers to apps like Explain Everything or Book Creator.

Task Card
innovatewithipad.com

The Task

One Is a Snail, Ten Is a Crab, written by April Pulley Sayre and Jeff Sayre and illustrated by Randy Cecil, is the perfect example of literature inspiring math. This colourful story explores the number of legs animals have (e.g., a snail has one leg, a person has two legs, an insect has six legs), and then combines those legs to create number sentences.

The Student's Learning Intention

- "I can show different ways to make a number."

The How

1. Read *One Is a Snail, Ten Is a Crab* and think about the animals and their legs.
2. Select a number and then answer this question: If there are [your number] of legs in the barn, who is in the barn?
3. Open your favourite drawing app.
4. Draw the animals whose legs, when combined, equal your number.
5. Save your work.

Bigger Than a Baby, Smaller Than an Elephant

The Task

In this open-ended lesson, students use their iPad's camera to take photos of body parts (hand, ear, arm, etc.) and compare them to the same body part on a baby or elephant.

The Student's Learning Intentions

- "I can compare the size of objects."
- "I can make statements of comparison."

The How

1. On your own or with a friend, use your iPad's camera to take photos of at least five of your body parts, such as your nose, hand, arm, foot, finger, or leg.
2. Open Book Creator.
3. Tap New Book (top left).
4. Choose your template.
5. Create your title page, being sure to include the headline "Bigger Than a Baby, Smaller Than an Elephant."
6. Create a new page and tap the "+" button to access your photos.
7. Add a photo of your body part.
8. Tap the "+" button again and select voice recording.
9. Look at your picture and record whether you think the body part is bigger than a baby's or smaller than an elephant's.
10. Repeat the process, creating a new page for each body part.
11. To modify or delete anything you have added, tap the "i" button.
12. Save your book.

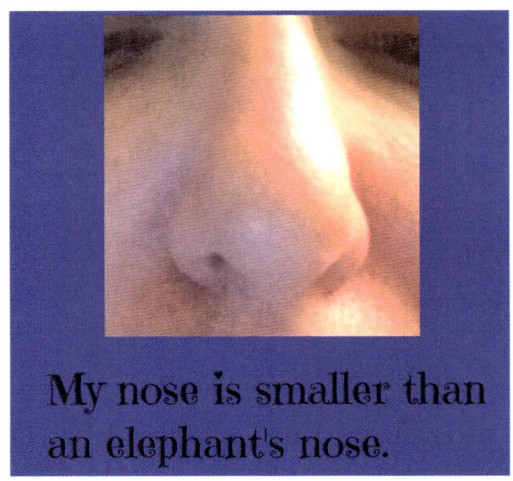

My nose is smaller than an elephant's nose.

Grade Level
K–1

Subject Area
Relative Size

iPad Comfort Level
Advanced

Suggested Apps
Book Creator
Explain Everything

Quick Tip

To modify or delete something, touch the "i" button. To add something to the page touch the "+" button. Each addition has its own options.

Lesson Extensions

Have students add text to each page of the book, explaining the relationship between their body part and the item they are comparing it to.

Designate a standard unit of measurement and have students measure the size of each of their body parts and then estimate (or research) the official size of that same body part on a baby or elephant.

Combinations of Twenty

Grade Level
1–2

Subject Area
Number Sense

iPad Comfort Level
Advanced

Suggested App
Number Frames

Quick Tip
Have students take a screenshot of their work and add it to a whiteboard app like Explain Everything so they can add their voice and thinking.

Lesson Extension
Once students find all of the possible solutions, give them a different number to explore. This is also an easy way to modify the lesson for different grades and student levels. For example, kindergarten students could start with a five frame, whereas first graders may start with a ten frame.

Task Card
innovatewithipad.com

The Task
In this open-ended problem, students use Number Frames to decompose numbers to twenty and learn about part-whole relationships.

The Student's Learning Intentions
- "I know how to use two number frames to make different combinations of twenty."
- "I can write the number sentence that goes with my picture."

The How
1. Answer the following question: If you have twenty blue and red counters, what could your ten frames look like?
2. Open Number Frames.
3. Choose two ten frames.
4. Fill your number frames with blue and red counters.
5. Write the corresponding number sentence that goes with the number frames.
6. Choose two more ten frames.
7. Fill your number frames with a different combination of red and blue counters.
8. Write the number sentence that goes with those number frames.
9. Create as many combinations as you can.
10. Take a screenshot of your work.

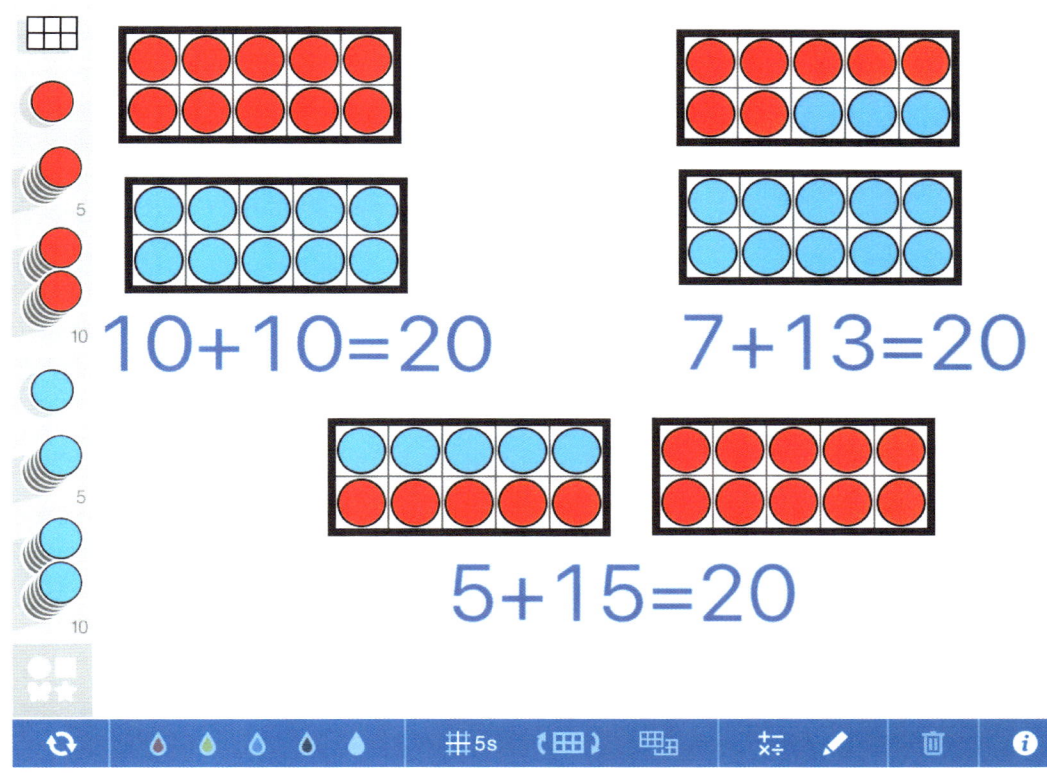

10+10=20

7+13=20

5+15=20

Farmyard Multiplication

Grade Level
2–3

Subject Area
Operations

iPad Comfort Level
Advanced

Suggested Apps
Make a Scene: Farmyard
Explain Everything

Task Card
innovatewithipad.com

The Task
This activity is a fun way for students to create and solve one-step multiplication problems using pictorial representations to calculate the answer.

The Student's Learning Intentions
- "I can represent a multiplication problem as repeated addition or groups."
- "I can recognize, create, and use arrays to represent multiplication."

The How
1. Open Make a Scene: Farmyard.
2. Choose a scene (top).
3. Use stickers (bottom) to create a multiplication problem.
4. Save your scene to the Camera Roll.
5. Open Explain Everything.
6. Add your farm scene.
7. Tap the text tool.
8. Write the number sentence for your scene.
9. Using the pen tool, circle the groups of items that make up your number sentence.
10. Record yourself explaining your thinking.
11. Export your video to the Camera Roll.

The Answer Is _____

Grade Level
1–3

Subject Area
Number Sense

iPad Comfort Level
Advanced

Suggested Apps
Book Creator
Number Pieces

Quick Tip
This activity can also be done in Explain Everything.

Lesson Extensions
Students can add a number sentence, use different manipulatives to answer the question in new ways, and experiment with subtraction to answer the question.

The Task
In this open-ended lesson, students show ways to make a specific number, such as twenty, one hundred, or one thousand (depending upon their grade level).

The Student's Learning Intentions
- "I can show different ways to make a number."
- "I can demonstrate that numbers are made up of parts."

The How
1. After discussing it with your teacher, select a number.
2. Answer this: How many different ways can you show the answer to the question, "If the answer is _____, what is the question?"
3. Using Number Pieces, create your number using units, rods, and flats.
4. Save the image to your iPad's Camera Roll.
5. Now create the same number using a new combination of units, rods, and flats.
6. Open your iPad's Book Creator app.
7. Tap New Book (top left).
8. Choose your template.
9. Create a title page with this headline: "The Answer Is _____. What Is the Question?" and put your number in place of the blank.
10. Create a new page and tap "+" (top right) to access your photos.
11. Add one of your number representations.
12. Write the number sentence to match your image.
13. Repeat the process as many times as necessary, creating a new page for each image.
14. Save your book.

The answer is 44, what is the question?

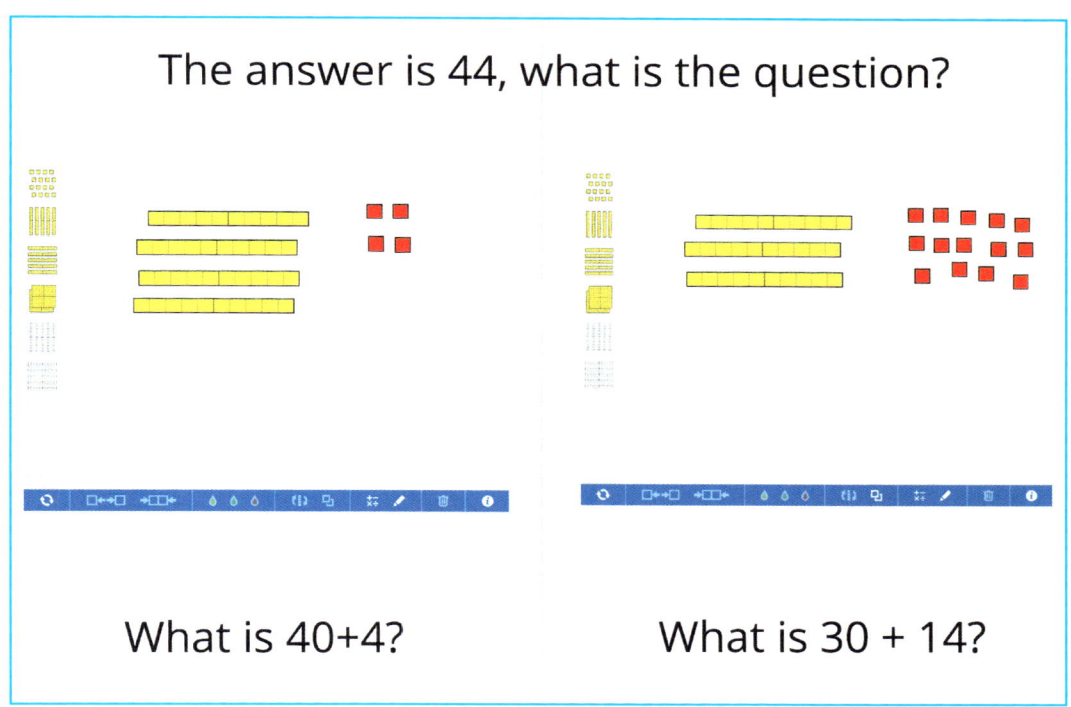

What is 40+4?   What is 30 + 14?

Composing and Decomposing Numbers Using Standard and Expanded Form

Grade Level
1–3

Subject Area
Number Sense

iPad Comfort Level
Advanced

Suggested Apps
Number Pieces
Popplet/Popplet Lite

Quick Tip
Instead of having students choose their own numbers, give them three dice to roll. Students must then make the largest or smallest number with the dice and show their numbers using Number Pieces and Popplet. For example if I rolled a two, four, and three, the largest number would be 432 and the smallest number would be 234.

Lesson Extension
This lesson can easily include numbers in the thousands.

Task Card
innovatewithipad.com

The Task
In this lesson, students compose and decompose numbers into the hundreds place as they move from standard to expanded form.

The Student's Learning Intentions
- "I build numbers up to the hundreds place with base ten blocks."
- "I compose and decompose numbers using standard and expanded form."
- "I use place value to compare the values of numbers."

The How
1. Open Number Pieces.
2. Choose two three-digit numbers.
3. Using base ten pieces, build the two numbers you have chosen.
4. Take a screenshot of each number.
5. Open Popplet.
6. Touch the screen to create a popple.
7. Add the two images that you created using Number Pieces.
8. Create two more popples.
9. Write the three-digit numbers in each popple.
10. Add two additional popples for each, showing the number you chose in the expanded form.
11. Add a final popple to compare the two numbers using the mathematical signs for less than, equal to, and more than.

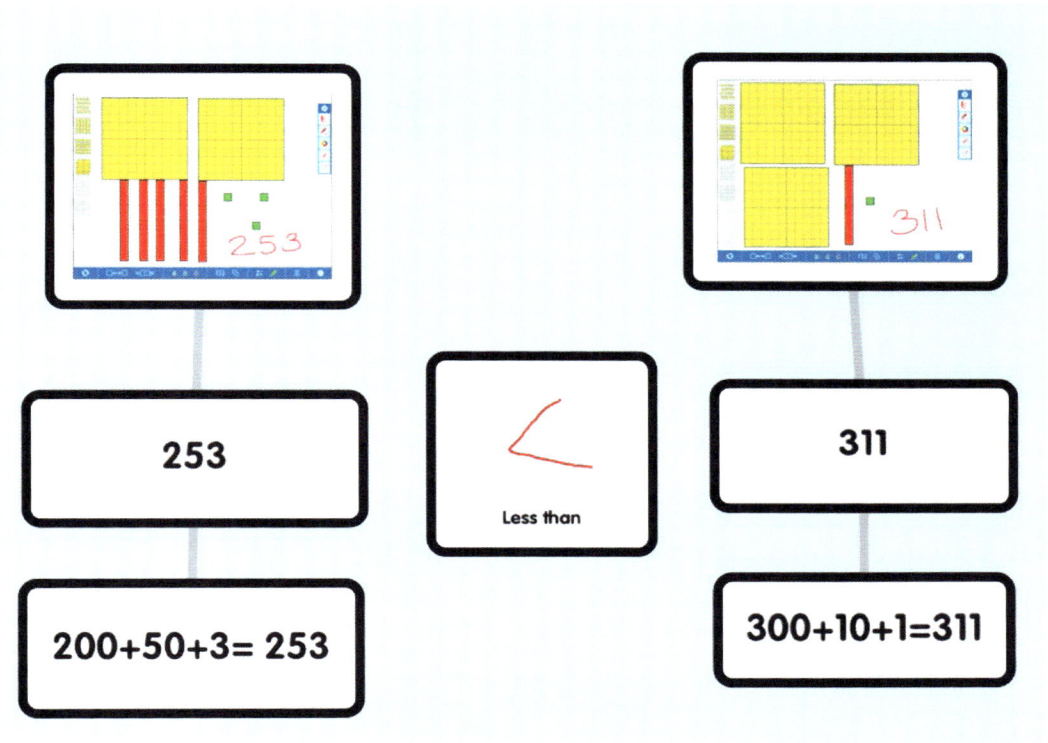

253

Less than

311

200+50+3= 253

300+10+1=311

Equivalent Fractions

Task Card

Grade Level
3

Subject Area
Fractions

iPad Comfort Level
Beginner

Suggested App
Geoboard

Lesson Extension
Using the Geoboard app, have students show fractions equivalent to one-quarter.

Task Card
innovatewithipad.com

The Task

This activity is a great way to help students visualize the concept that equivalent fractions are simply different fractions that name the same number.

The Student's Learning Intention

- "I identify and represent equivalent fractions using concrete objects."

The How

1. Open Geoboard.
2. Answer the following question: How many different ways can you represent the fraction one-half?
3. Draw as many ways to show fractions equivalent to one-half as you can using Geoboard.
4. Using the rubber bands, create fractions equivalent to one-half.
5. Write the fraction beside your picture.
6. Save your work.

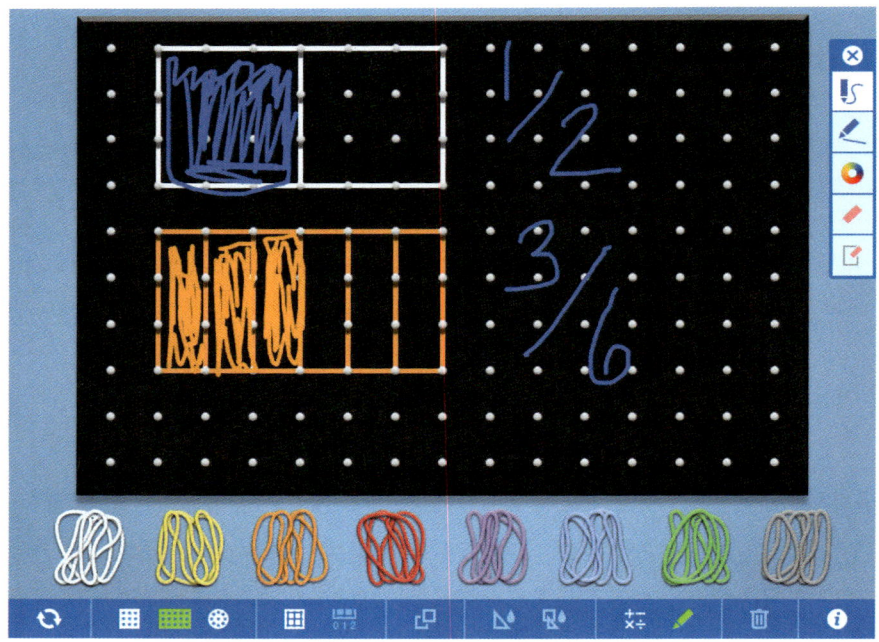

The Task

Addition leads to a total and subtraction indicates what's missing. In this open-ended activity, students use money, addition, and subtraction to create their problem and solve it.

The Student's Learning Intentions

- "I can choose an amount of money that I have in my pocket."
- "I can pretend that I have a hole in my pocket and lose twenty-six cents."
- "I can figure out how much I started with."
- "I know how much I have left."

The How

1. Open Explain Everything.
2. Choose an amount of money to start with.
3. Use manipulatives, pictures, and numbers to show how much money you started with.
4. Now, show how much money you have left after losing twenty-six cents.
5. Write a number sentence to describe what happened.
6. Record yourself explaining your thinking.
7. Export your video to your iPad's Camera Roll.

Grade Level

2–3

Subject Areas

Money, Addition, and Subtraction

iPad Comfort Level

Advanced

Suggested App

Explain Everything

Quick Tip

Students could use manipulatives (play money) to help them solve the problem. Have students take a picture of their manipulatives and then import it into Explain Everything, where they can visualize their thinking.

Lesson Extension

This lesson can be done several times by the same student because the question ("How much do I have left?") changes when the starting amount changes. Challenge students to try the activity using larger dollar amounts.

Task Card

innovatewithipad.com

My Hand Is Smaller/Bigger Than {iMovie}

The Task

Students use the iPad camera and iMovie to capture and document items larger and smaller than their hands.

The Student's Learning Intention

- "I can identify items in my environment larger and smaller than my hand."

The How

1. Trace your hand on a scrap piece of paper and cut it out.
2. Using your iPad, take photos of your paper hand beside bigger and smaller things.
3. Open iMovie.
4. Tap Projects.
5. Tap the "+" to add a new project.
6. Select Movie.
7. Choose a movie template and tap Create. (It is best to use the "Simple" template if you're new to iMovie.)
8. Once you are in the movie, tap Photos or Video to choose which images and videos you want to use.
9. As you select an image or video, you will see a small arrow. Tap this arrow and your selection will drop into the video working area.
10. To add text and a title to your movie, touch an image and press the Titles section.
11. If you want to add a voice recording, select the image you would like to add your voice to and press the microphone.
12. To extend your image, select it and then drag the thicker yellow image markers to the right or left.
13. When your project is complete, tap Done.
14. Save your movie to the iPad Camera Roll.

The Task

Students use Popplet and their iPad's camera to capture and document shapes they find in their environment.

The Student's Learning Intention

- "I can identify shapes in my environment."

The How

1. Using the camera on your iPad, take photos of a specific shape you see in the classroom.
2. Open Popplet.
3. Touch the screen to create a popple.
4. Use the text feature (bottom) and write your popplet's title. For example, "Cylinders in My Classroom."
5. Add more popples, adding a photo of the shape in your environment to each.
6. Once you have finished your popplet, tap Export to save or share it.

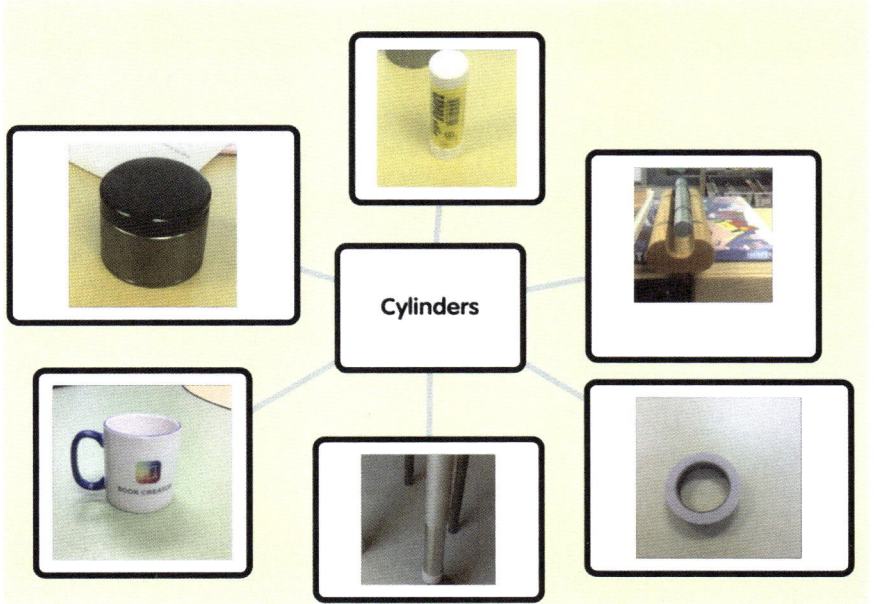

Grade Level

K–3

Subject Area

Geometric Shapes

iPad Comfort Level

Beginner

Suggested App

Popplet/Popplet Lite

Quick Tip

You can connect popples by dragging the grey circle from one popplet to the next.

Lesson Extensions

Depending on your students' age, have them look for objects with four sides, specific two- and three-dimensional shapes and solids, or items with similar attributes.

The popplet could also be used to add multiple shapes found in the classroom. For example, a popplet which includes spheres, cylinders, and rectangular prisms.

Centimetres or Metres?

Grade Level
2

Subject Area
Measurement

iPad Comfort Level
Beginner

Suggested App
Pic Collage

Lesson Extension
You could easily change this lesson to illustrate different units of measurement, including nonstandard ones.

Task Card
innovatewithipad.com

The Task

As students investigate and take photos of items in your classroom, they decide whether centimetres or metres would be the best unit of measurement for each object. This lesson helps students develop an understanding of the size of a centimetre and metre.

The Student's Learning Intentions

- "I understand the size of a standard unit of measurement."
- "I estimate using centimetres and metres."
- "I choose the best standard unit to use based on an object's size."

The How

1. Using your iPad, take photos of at least six different objects in the classroom that you would measure with either centimetres or metres.
2. Open Pic Collage.
3. Press "+" to start a new collage.
4. Tap the "+" (bottom) and select a maximum of twelve photos.
5. Tap the checkmark (top right corner) to add your images to your collage.
6. At this point, you can choose to either organize your images freehand or use a template. To access Pic Collage's templates, tap the grid square (bottom left) and select the grid that works best with your images.
7. Tap the "+" again and select the Text button. Label your picture with "cm" for centimetres or "m" for metres.
8. Add your name to your work.
9. To save your image, press the box with the arrow pointing outward. This will automatically save your collage to the Camera Roll, but if you would like to share it on social media, via email, or to your Google Drive, select the appropriate option.

Centimetres or Metres?

Area and Perimeter Math Challenge

Grade Level
2–3

Subject Area
Measurement

iPad Comfort Level
Advanced

Suggested Apps
Geoboard
Explain Everything

Quick Tip
If you tap the fourth image along the bottom of the Geoboard app, the board's gridlines will appear

Lesson Extension
Ask your students to create four different shapes with the same perimeter or area. For example, if each square on the geoboard is one centimetre, create four different figures on the geoboard that all have a perimeter of twenty centimetres.

Task Card
innovatewithipad.com

The Task
Geoboard lets your students explore shapes and the mathematical concepts of perimeter and area using virtual rubber bands that won't fly across your classroom.

The Student's Learning Intentions
- "I know the number of square units needed to cover a surface's area."
- "I understand that the sum of the lengths of a shape's sides is its perimeter."
- "I can calculate a random shape's area and perimeter on a grid."

The How
1. Open Geoboard.
2. Using the app's rubber bands, create four different-coloured figures.
3. Take a screenshot of your two-dimensional figures.
4. Open Explain Everything.
5. Start a new project.
6. Choose the + sign and add an existing picture from the Camera Roll.
7. Select your screenshot.
8. Label each figure's area and perimeter.

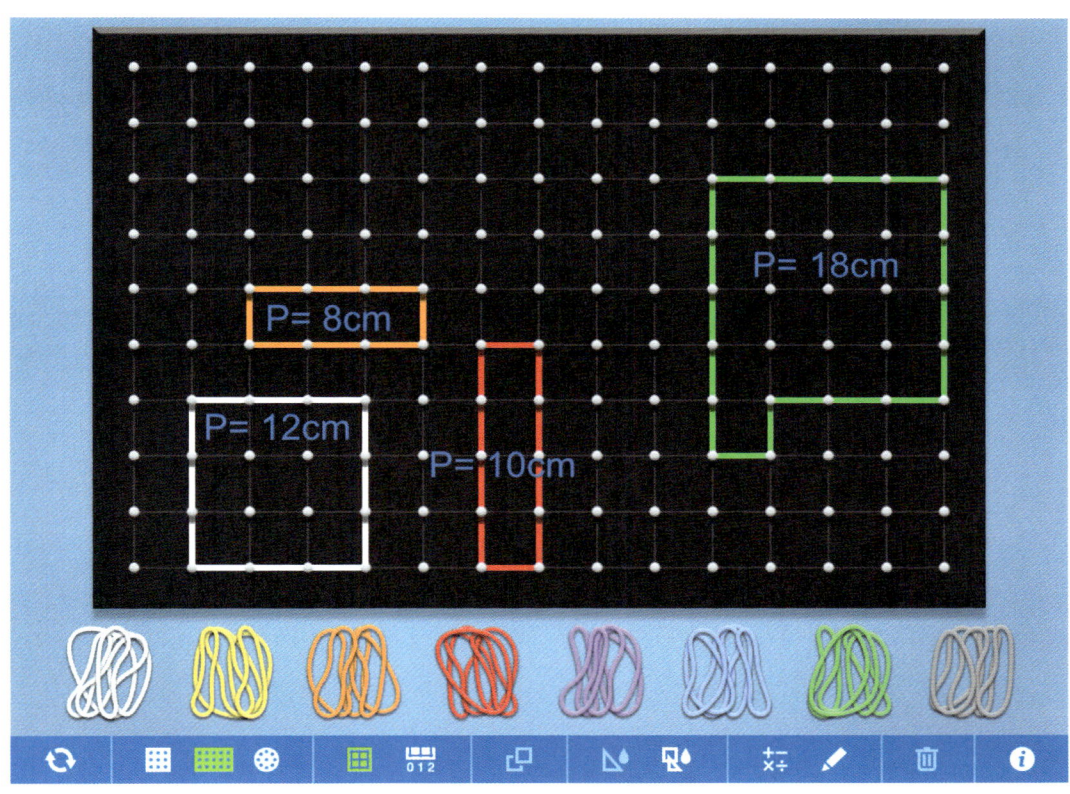

Making One Dollar Four Different Ways

Grade Level
1–3

Subject Area
Measurement (Money)

iPad Comfort Level
Beginner

Suggested App
Draw and Tell

Lesson Extension
Have students choose a different money amount and repeat the process

Task Card
innovatewithipad.com

Student Example
innovatewithipad.com

The Task

This lesson helps students learn the relative value of a penny, nickel, dime, quarter, and dollar by creating different combinations to equal one dollar.

The Student's Learning Intention

- "I can show how to make one dollar four different ways using manipulatives."

The How

1. Using a math organizer and money manipulatives, show one dollar four different ways.
2. Take a picture of your work with your iPad's camera.
3. Open the Draw and Tell App.
4. Choose New Drawing.
5. Select the upload picture option and choose your images to upload.
6. Record yourself explaining your work.
7. Save your video to the Camera Roll.

The Task

In this open-ended activity, students pay close attention to figures' attributes by creating and sorting like shapes.

The Student's Learning Intention

- "I can sort shapes using one or more attributes."

The How

1. Open Geoboard.
2. Select the large grid (bottom).
3. Choose a rubber band and create a line down the middle of the grid.
4. Select an attribute, such as colour, number of sides, or corners, to sort shapes by.
5. Create shapes based on your attribute rule for both sides of the middle line.
6. Take a screenshot to save your work.

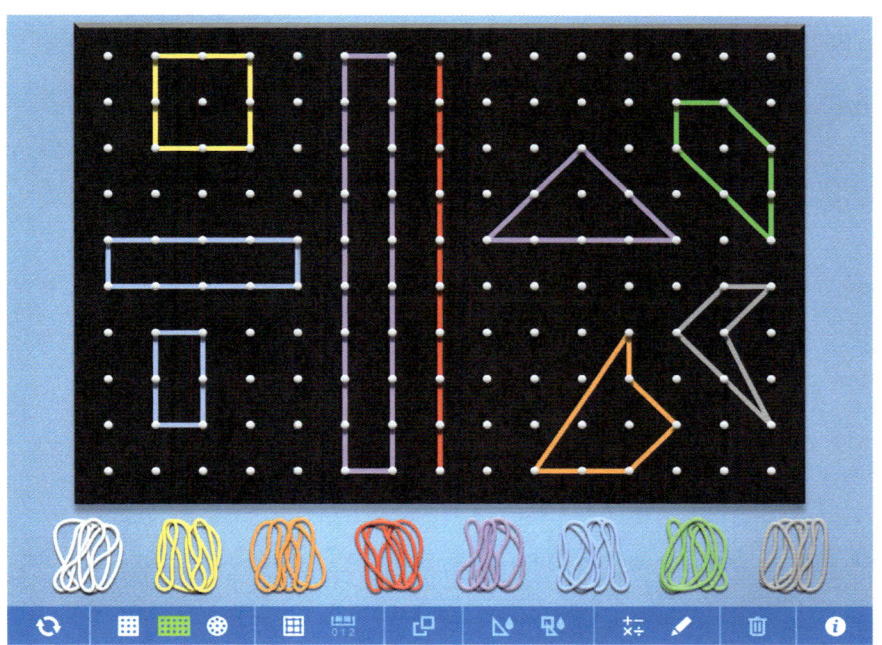

Grade Level

1–2

Subject Area

Shapes' Attributes

iPad Comfort Level

Advanced

Suggested App

Geoboard

Lesson Extensions

Challenge students to sort their shapes using two or more attributes.

Require your students to annotate their image by adding their sorting rule(s).

Have the class upload their screenshots to Explain Everything and record themselves explaining their thinking behind the sort.

3-D Shapes in My Environment {iMovie}

Grade Level
K–2

Subject Area
Geometry

iPad Comfort Level
Beginner

Suggested App
iMovie

Quick Tip
Have your students take images of four different shapes.

Lesson Extension
Ask students to take pictures of both 3-D shapes and the 2-D shapes that comprise them.

Student Example
innovatewithipad.com

The Task
iMovie is the perfect app for students to use to create a movie showcasing their images of three-dimensional shapes in their environment. The app is open-ended enough to allow all learners to be successful.

The Student's Learning Intention
• "I can identify 3-D shapes in my environment."

The How
1. Go on a shape hunt in your classroom and, using your iPad, take photos of the shapes you see.
2. Open iMovie.
3. Tap Projects.
4. Tap the "+" button to add a new project.
5. Select Movie.
6. Pick the movie template you want to use and then tap Create. (If you are new to iMovie, the "Simple" template is the best option.)
7. Once you are in the movie, touch Photos to add the images you took.
8. Tap the checkmarks to select the images you want to add to your project, and they will drop into the video working area.
9. To add text to your images, touch an image and then press the "Titles" section.
10. Add your title text.
11. To add a voiceover identifying the object in the image, select the image you want to add your voice to and tap the microphone to start recording.
12. Adjust the size of your images, selecting each image and then dragging the thicker yellow image markers to the right or left.
13. When your project is done, tap Done and save your movie to the iPad's Camera Roll.

The Task

This lesson activity reviews 3-D shapes and introduces the activity of creating riddles to identify the attributes of the shape.

The Student's Learning Intention

• "I use geometric language to describe 3-D solids' attributes."

The How

1. Choose a three-dimensional solid.
2. Examine and describe it.
   - How many sides or faces does it have?
   - Does it have a curved surface?
   - Does it have vertices (corners)? How many?
   - Does it stack or roll?
3. Take a picture of your solid.
4. Open Explain Everything.
5. Choose a background and insert your picture.
6. Write three clues about your solid.
7. Take another photo, this time of a background that you want to use to hide the picture of your solid.
8. Crop the background picture so that it covers your solid.
9. Record yourself reading your clues, pausing five seconds after the last one before sliding the background picture off to reveal your solid.

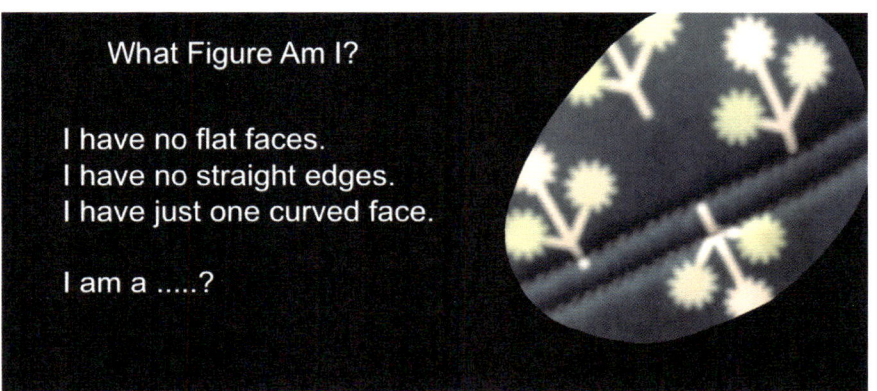

Grade Level

2–3

Subject Area

Geometry

iPad Comfort Level

Advanced

Suggested App

Explain Everything

Quick Tip

When you ask students to do a more complicated or a multi-step project on their iPad, include a QR code that links to an example of the finished product. This way, if students get confused or have questions, they can scan the QR code and attempt to find their answer before coming to you.

Task Card

innovatewithipad.com

Student Example

innovatewithipad.com

Telling Time to the Hour

Grade Level
K–1

Subject Area
Measurement

iPad Comfort Level
Beginner

Suggested Apps
Geoboard
Draw and Tell

Quick Tip
Students could also use Explain Everything instead of Draw and Tell for this activity

Lesson Extension
Ask students to show half-hours using the geoboard. For example, "Can you show me 3:30 on the geoboard?"

Task Card
innovatewithipad.com

The Task

Teaching time to the hour can be tricky for some young children. By using two different colours for the hands of the clock, this will help children distinguish between the hour and minute hands. Students will soon realize in this activity that the red hand (minute hand) always stays pointing to the "12" when reading the time to the hour, and the yellow hand (hour hand) is the hand that they move to tell the time to each hour.

The Student's Learning Intention

- "I can tell and write the time to the hour."

The How

1. Open Geoboard.
2. Select the circle grid picture from the menu underneath the geoboard.
3. Write the hours around your clock.
4. Using the red and yellow rubber bands, red for the minute hand (long) and yellow for the hour hand (short), show 3:00.
5. Take a screenshot.
6. Now do the same for the following times, saving each:

    6:00   9:00   12:00

7. Open the Draw and Tell app.
8. Choose Blank Paper, then the picture with the two grids.
9. Select your first screenshot.
10. Tap the microphone (top right), and record yourself saying the time that your clock shows.
11. Tap the save arrow.
12. Repeat the process until all four slides are saved.
13. Drag and drop one scene onto another to create a group. By creating a group, you will now be able to save all of your slides as one video.
14. Save the entire group.

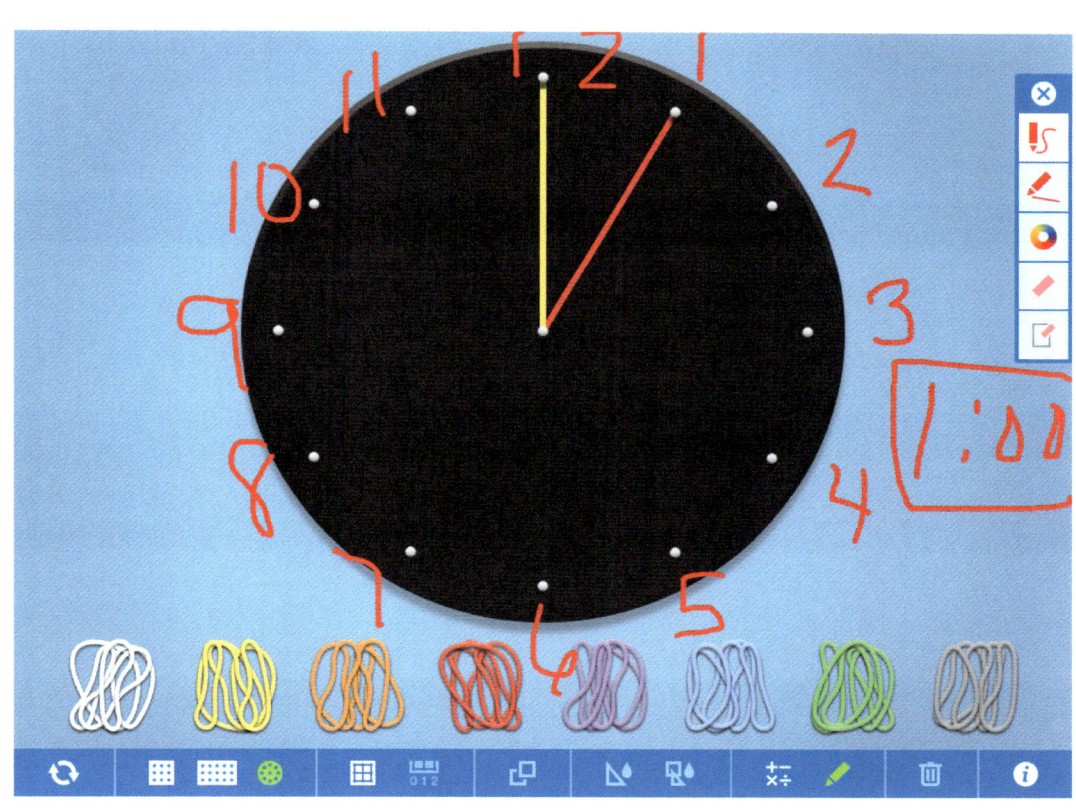

3-D Scavenger Hunt

Grade Level
2–3

Subject Area
Geometry

iPad Comfort Level
Beginner

Suggested App
Pic Collage

Quick Tip
For reference, post an anchor chart in your classroom with the correct spelling of each 3-D solid your students are using in their collage.

Task Card
innovatewithipad.com

The Task
This is a wonderful activity for your students to do in your classroom, around their school, or on the playground. Students take pictures of and label three-dimensional solids they find in their environment, solidifying their understanding of three-dimensional solids.

The Student's Learning Intention
- "I can find and name 3-D solids in my environment."

The How
1. Use your iPad to take photos of at least five different three-dimensional solids that you find around your school.
2. Open Pic Collage.
3. Press "+" to start a new collage.
4. Tap the "+" (bottom) and select a maximum of twelve photos.
5. Tap the checkmark (top right corner of each photo) to add your images to your collage.
6. Label your photos with the correct 3-D solid's name.
7. Add your name to your work.
8. To save your image, press the box with the arrow pointing outward. This will automatically save your collage to the Camera Roll, but if you would like to share it on social media, via email, or to your Google Drive, select the appropriate option.

Comparing 3-D Solids

Grade Level
2–3

Subject Area
Geometry

iPad Comfort Level
Beginner

Suggested App
Explain Everything

Quick Tip
Keep solid-coloured scrap paper on hand for students to use as a background for their pictures. This ensures your students will have a clean, clutter-free background for their images.

Lesson Extension
Have students choose three solids to compare.

Task Card
innovatewithipad.com

The Task
In this activity, students look at two three-dimensional solids' differences and similarities. Students then label the solids and use their voice to answer prompts.

The Student's Learning Intention
• "I can compare and identify 3-D solids."

The How
1. Choose two solids.
2. Look at your solids and determine which attributes (e.g., faces, edges, or vertices) are the same and which ones are different.
3. Take one photo that includes both figures.
4. Open Explain Everything.
5. Insert your picture.
6. Label your photo with the solids' names.
7. Record yourself answering these questions:
    • How is your solid the same as the other solid?
    • How is it different?
8. Save your work to the iPad's Camera Roll.

The Task

Students will love taking pictures of their classroom and searching for two- and three-dimensional shapes in the picture. This reinforces geometric language and finding real-world shapes in their environment.

The Student's Learning Intention

- "I can find and name two- and three-dimensional shapes in our classroom."

The How

1. Using your iPad's camera, take a photo of an area in your classroom.
2. Open Draw and Tell.
3. Choose the blank paper option and then the picture option.
4. Select the photo you took.
5. Tap the paintbrush tool to draw.
6. Find two 2-D and two 3-D figures in your picture.
7. Trace the figures on the picture to show where you found them.
8. Tap the microphone button and record yourself explaining your thinking, being sure to include each figure's name.
9. Save your work.

Grade Level
K–2

Subject Area
Geometry

iPad Comfort Level
Beginner

Suggested App
Draw and Tell

Quick Tip
You can modify this activity to fit your students' needs. If students are just learning basic shapes, then you could have students only focus on 2-D shapes.

Task Card
innovatewithipad.com

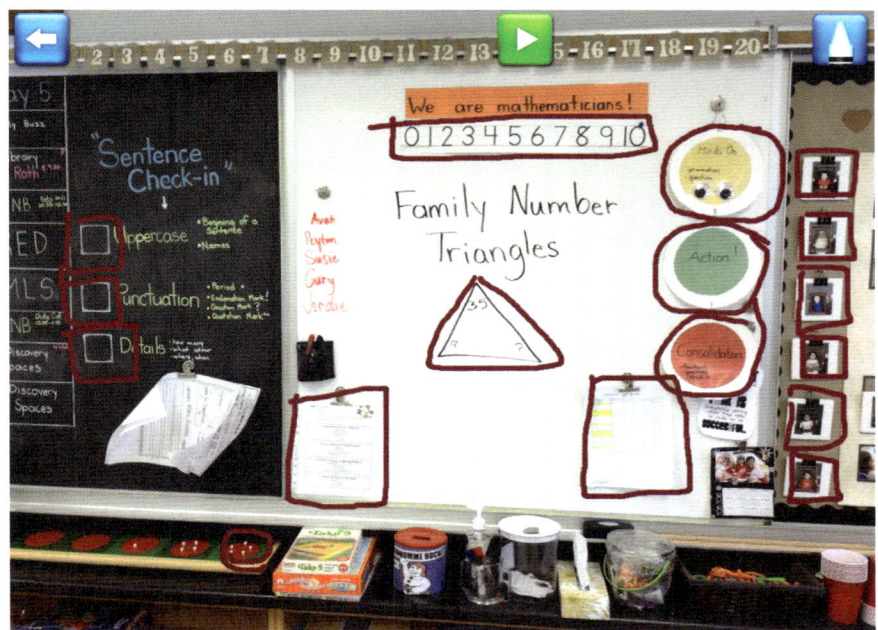

chapter three
Literacy Lessons

iPad has transformed literacy programs by allowing young learners to create in ways not previously possible. The following lessons are designed to help your students find innovative ways to develop, practice, and demonstrate their literacy skills.

Drawing to Capture the Main Idea

Grade Level

K–3

Subject Area

Reading Comprehension

iPad Comfort Level

Beginner

Suggested Apps

Drawing Pad
Doodle Buddy
Drawing App of
   Your Choice

Lesson Extensions

Students can use this strategy when reading text independently.

If they're able, have students add text to their drawings or take a screen shot and add a voice recording so they can better explain their creations.

The Task

Like us, we're sure you've found many students learn best when they draw meaningful images. That's because creating a representation of an idea requires the student to process the information they've read and heard. Now, with the help of their iPads, even your youngest learners can share a story's main idea.

The Student's Learning Intention

- "I can draw the main idea of a story."

The How

1. Open your favourite drawing app.
2. Listen to your teacher read a story. As you listen, think about the story's main idea.
3. Begin drawing the main idea while your teacher is reading.
4. Finish your drawing as the story ends.
5. Save it to the iPad's Camera Roll.

Created by Sajjad S. Surrey, BC, Canada

Using Drawing Pad to Make Predictions

The Task

Through the creation of an image, your youngest learners can better process what they're reading or hearing and predict what will happen in a story.

The Student's Learning Intention

• "I can draw my prediction of what I think will happen next."

The How

1. Open your favourite drawing app on your iPad.
2. Listen to your teacher read the story to the class and think about what is happening.
3. When your teacher pauses, make a prediction—draw what you think will happen next.
4. Share your drawing with a classmate or your teacher.
5. Save your drawing to the Camera Roll.

Grade Level

K–3

Subject Area

Reading Comprehension

iPad Comfort Level

Beginner

Suggested Apps

Drawing Pad
Doodle Buddy
Drawing App of
  Your Choice

Lesson Extensions

Depending upon your students' learning level, you could have them either add text to their drawing or take a screenshot of it and use a voice-recording app to explain their thinking.

I think she will find the ring under the rock.

Making Connections Using Drawing Pad

Grade Level
K–3

Subject Area
Reading Comprehension

iPad Comfort Level
Beginner

Suggested Apps
Drawing Pad
Doodle Buddy
Drawing App of
Your Choice

Lesson Extensions
You can have students apply this strategy while reading text independently.

If they can, your students can add text to their drawings or take screenshots and record themselves explaining their creations.

The Task

Students will use a drawing app to draw their connection to a story. The three main types of connections are: text-self, text-text, and text-world. In text to self, the student would draw how something they read or heard in the story connects to them personally. For example, the main character has a dog, and they have a dog, too. In text-text, the student would connect the story they are listening to or reading to a story they have already read or heard. For example, a story about the fire station reminds them of a story about a fire truck. In text-world, the student would connect the story to something they have seen happen in the world, but not necessarily to them specifically. For example, in a story about a panda, they might remember seeing a panda on the news.

The Student's Learning Intention

- "I can draw a connection to the story."

The How

1. Open your favourite drawing app.
2. Listen to your teacher read the story.
3. Think about a connection you have to the story. The three types of connections you may have are text to self, text to text, or text to world.
4. Draw your connection.
5. Save your drawing to the iPad's Camera Roll.

Just like Sally in the book I like pepperoni and mushroom pizza too.

New/Knew: A Thinking Strategy

The Task

Whether a student is reading text for the first time, being read to, or watching a movie, it's important for them to be able to identify the information they knew about a topic before combining it with what they're learning. Drawing out their understanding is a great way for a student to process their learning visually.

The Student's Learning Intentions

- "I can identify what I know about a given topic."
- "I can identify the information I'm learning about a given topic."

The How

1. Listen to your teacher read a non-fiction book, paying close attention to what you already know about the topic and what the book is teaching you.
2. Open your favourite drawing app.
3. Divide the page in half.
4. Label one side "Knew" and the other side "New."
5. Draw what you learned on the "New" side and what you already knew on the "Knew" side.
6. Save your work to the iPad's Camera Roll.

Created by Mya L. Surrey, BC, Canada

Grade Level
K–3

Subject Area
Reading Comprehension

iPad Comfort Level
Beginner

Suggested Apps
Draw and Tell
Drawing Pad
Drawing App of
    Your Choice

Lesson Extensions

To further show what they already knew and what they learned, ask students to either add text to their drawings or import their drawings and then record their thinking in an app such as Draw and Tell or Explain Everything.

Encourage students to draw the new information they are learning as they listen to you read the story.

It Begins with the Letter...

Grade Level
K

Subject Area
Phonemic Awareness

iPad Comfort Level
Beginner

Suggested Apps
Pic Collage
Explain Everything

Quick Tip
Have your students take all of their photos before opening Pic Collage. It's easier for little ones to manage doing one thing at a time.

Lesson Extensions
You can easily adapt this lesson for rhyming words, ending letter sounds, and syllables.

Task Card
innovatewithipad.com

The Task

This is an easy and fun way for students to show you they understand their beginning letter sounds. In this activity, ask students to take pictures of items in the classroom that begin with the letter of your choosing.

The Student's Learning Intention

• "I can find things in my classroom that begin with a specific letter."

The How

1. Use your iPad to take photos of at least five different things in the classroom that begin with the letter ___.
2. Open Pic Collage.
3. Import your pictures.
4. Title your project "It Begins with the Letter _____" and put your letter in place of the blank line.
5. Save your collage to the iPad's Camera Roll.

It begins with the letter P.

Word Families with Popplet

The Task

Introducing word families (e.g., the "-at" family would contain words like: fat, mat, cat, sat, etc.) is an efficient way to teach younger students the predictable spelling patterns in words. Once they understand these patterns, learners can easily decode words.

The Student's Learning Intentions

- "I recognize, read, and write word families."
- "I use letter patterns to create new words."
- "I read words that have similar patterns with fluency."

The How

1. Open Popplet.
2. Tap the screen to create a popple.
3. Along the bottom of the popple, add text.
4. Type the word _____.
5. Add a picture that is part of the word family (tap the picture icon) if you wish.
6. Tap one of the grey circles with white circles inside of it to add another popple.
7. Type a word that rhymes with _____.
8. Continue adding words that rhyme with your chosen word family.
9. Once you are finished, tap "Export" to save your popplet to the Camera Roll.

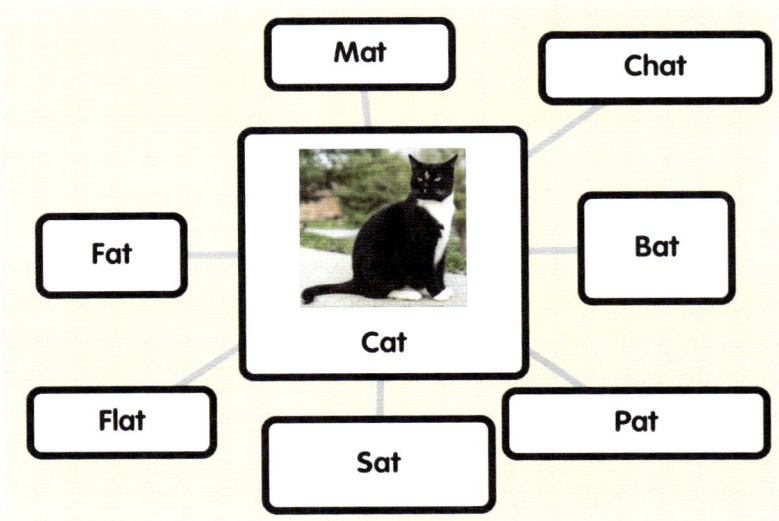

Grade Level

K–1

Subject Area

Phonemic Awareness

iPad Comfort Level

Beginner

Suggested App

Popplet

Quick Tip

Engaging in this activity with a small group of students is a great way to introduce Popplet. Once your small group can use the app fluently, put them to work showing their classmates how to use it.

Lesson Extensions

Create a bin with either Dr. Seuss books or other ones that focus on word families. Students can then look for word families that they can make graphic organizers for.

Task Card

innovatewithipad.com

Picture a Noun Literacy Station

Grade Level
1–3

Subject Area
Literacy

iPad Comfort Level
Beginner

Suggested App
Popplet/Popplet Lite

Quick Tip
It's easiest to have students take all of their pictures first and then import everything into Popplet at one time.

Lesson Extension
Have students open their saved popplet in Explain Everything and record themselves explaining it.

Task Card
innovatewithipad.com

The Task
This lesson introduces students to the concept that nouns are things that can be seen and touched. Using Popplet, students take pictures of nouns they find in their classroom and school.

The Student's Learning Intentions
- "I can explain that a noun is a person, place, or thing."
- "I can identify a noun as a person, place, or thing."
- "I can make a list of nouns (people, places, and things)."

The How
1. Open Popplet.
2. Name your popplet "Nouns" and choose a colour for it.
3. Create three popples and label them with these titles: "Person," "Place," and "Thing."
4. Add at least three pictures and words under each popple.
5. Export your popplet and save it as a JPEG.

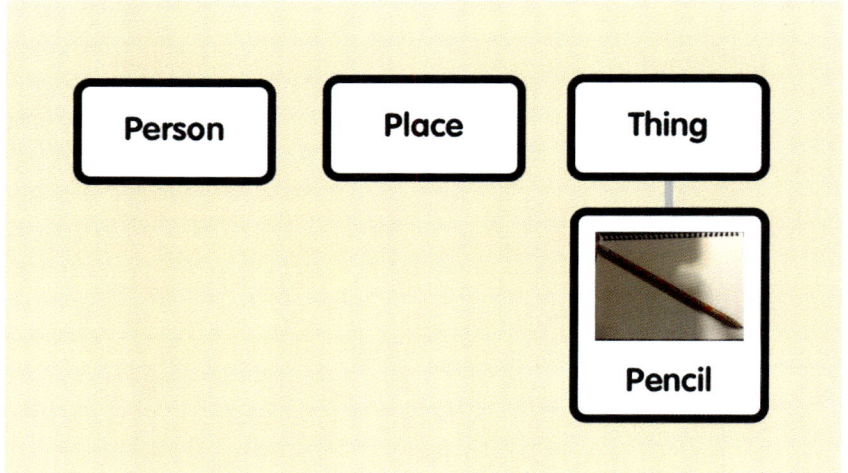

Thinking Critically During Non-Fiction Read-Alouds

The Task

As you read non-fiction texts aloud to your class, depending upon their age and ability, encourage your students to sketch and add notes to their pictures. Sketching while you read aloud teaches students to associate the pictures in their heads with the text you're reading, creating meaning. Younger students can add labels or record their thinking using an app like Explain Everything.

The Student's Learning Intentions

- "I can draw facts that I learn from the read-aloud."
- "I can jot down facts to go with my drawings."
- "I can label my drawings."

The How

1. Open Drawing Pad.
2. Listen to your teacher read the non-fiction book.
3. When you hear new learning, something interesting, or an important fact, sketch a picture of it.
4. Add labels or facts to your drawings.
5. For each new fact, start a new page.
6. Save your pages to your iPad's Camera Roll.

Frogs can ley 20,000 eggs. That's a lot of eggs!

Grade Level

K–3

Subject Area

Reading Comprehension

iPad Comfort Level

Beginner

Suggested App

Drawing Pad

Quick Tip

Encourage students to use the different backgrounds the Drawing Pad app provides to make their pictures pop.

Lesson Extension

If this is an ongoing topic of inquiry, students could import their pages into an app such as Book Creator and create a book with all of their pages.

Generating Ideas with Popplet

Grade Level
1–3

Subject Area
Writing

iPad Comfort Level
Beginner

Suggested App
Popplet

Quick Tip
Quickly share images with your class using AirDrop.

Lesson Extension
Have students use the ideas they brainstormed in their popplet to write about the prompt picture.

Task Card
innovatewithipad.com

The Task
Many young authors can write and write and write, but do not focus on one topic. This activity will help young writers to organize their thoughts and make sure they have enough details to create a descriptive story.

The Student's Learning Intention
- "I generate ideas for my writing using prewriting strategies (mind mapping and webs)."

The How
1. Use the camera to take a picture of the prompt your teacher provided.
2. Save it to your iPad's Camera Roll.
3. Open Popplet.
4. Touch your iPad screen to create a popple.
5. Tap the picture icon along the bottom of the popple and add the picture prompt.
6. Press one of the grey circles with white circles to add another popple.
7. Brainstorm possible ideas for the image your teacher provided.
8. Remember to include the five Ws (one for each popple):

   Who   What   Where   When   Why

9. Continue creating popples as needed.
10. Save your work to the Camera Roll.

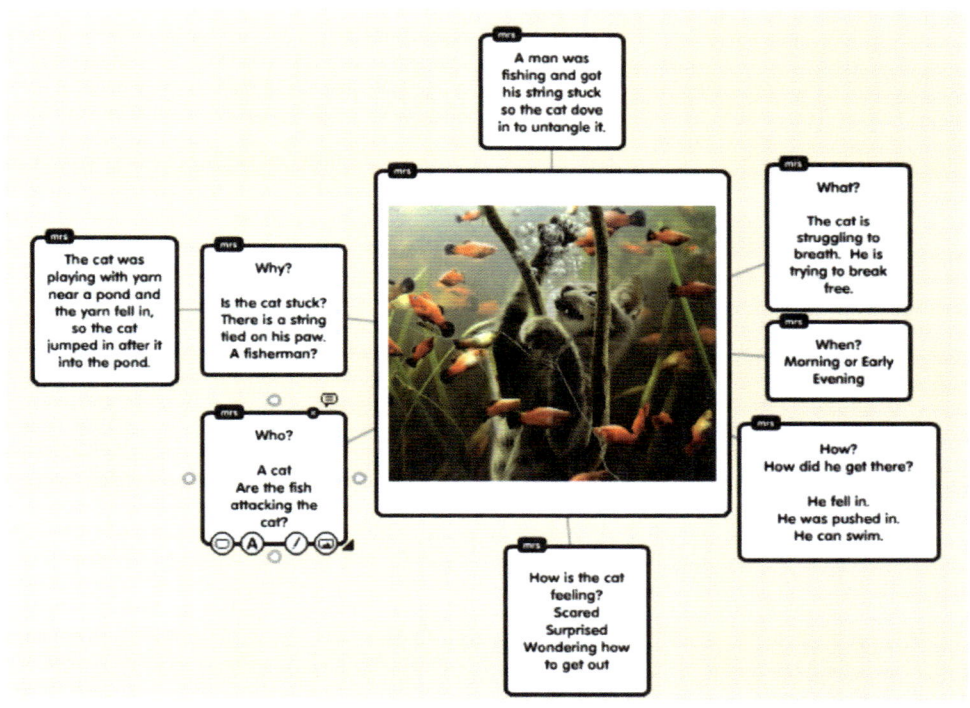

Non-Fiction Text Features Hunt

Grade Level
1-3

Subject Area
Literacy

iPad Comfort Level
Beginner

Suggested App
Pic Collage

The Task
This lesson encourages students to explore the organizational features of non-fiction texts by going on a scavenger hunt with their iPad and a few non-fiction books.

The Student's Learning Intention
- "I can find and identify different features in a non-fiction text."

The How
1. Use your iPad to take photos of these non-fiction books' text features:
   - Table of Contents
   - Photographs
   - Glossary
   - Bold Words
   - Index
   - Diagrams
   - Captions
2. After you have taken all of your photos, open Pic Collage.
3. Import your pictures.
4. Label them with the correct text feature name.
5. Save your collage.

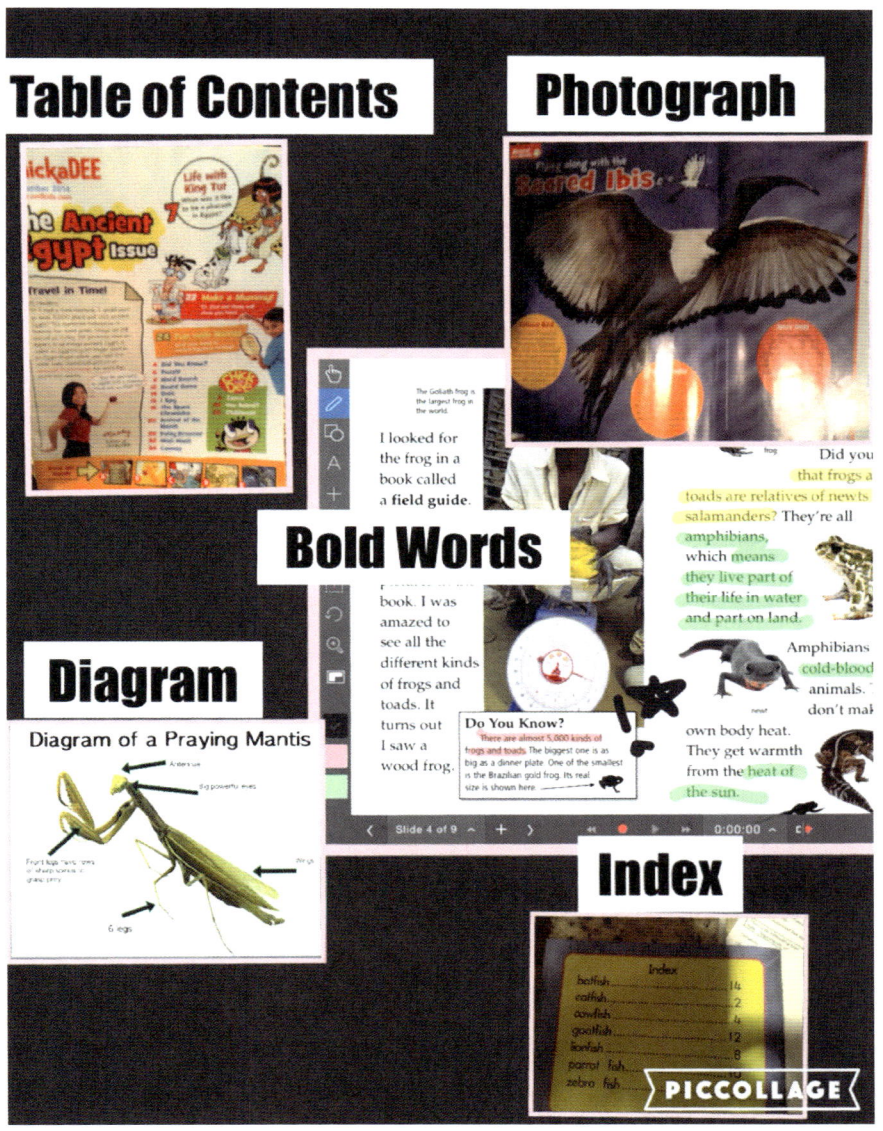

Table of Contents

Photograph

Bold Words

Diagram

Diagram of a Praying Mantis

Index

Using Drawing Pad to Show Student Thinking

Grade Level

K–3

Subject Area

Reading and Writing Informational Texts

iPad Comfort Level

Beginner

Suggested App

Drawing Pad

Quick Tips

If you have a class set of iPads, all of your students can draw while you're reading the text aloud. If you have one iPad for every two students, have your students work in pairs. If you have fewer iPads, model the strategy and then leave the book you read aloud in a literacy centre with the two or three iPads you do have.

Even if your students can't read yet, they can still look through the book and retell it in their own words.

Choose a book full of beautiful pictures, labels, and charts so that your students can complete this task while you're working with a small group elsewhere.

The Task

In this activity, you (the teacher) demonstrate for your class how to respond to content using a digital tool. Simply read an exciting non-fiction text aloud. After every couple of pages, stop and draw something you find interesting using your iPad's drawing app. Depending upon your students' age, you could even add text to your pictures.

The Student's Learning Intentions

- "I can listen to or read non-fiction texts and make notes about the content using either sketches or words."
- "I remember what I hear or read about during a lesson."

The How

1. Choose an exciting non-fiction book to read aloud. (Steve Jenkins' books are great for this activity.)
2. Read a couple of pages in the book.
3. Stop and model how to think aloud.
4. Using Apple TV or a projector to display your iPad screen, open Drawing Pad.
5. Draw a picture that represents the information you just shared with your class. Depending upon your students' learning level, you could add a word, sentence, or paragraph.
6. Save your image.
7. Open a fresh page.
8. Read a couple more pages and then repeat the drawing process.
9. Invite students to open Drawing Pad on their iPads and draw what they find interesting while you read the next few pages.

Megabats

Posted by: RyanL September 24, 2014 @ 9:40 AM   0 Comments

Bats
Mega bats eat fruit. They live in warm tropical places. The biggest megabat is the Malayan flying fox. It is as big as a bathtub.

Today we learned that megabats eat fruit.

Lesson Extension

Students of all abilities enjoy using drawing apps. Build upon Drawing Pad by having your students export their pictures into other apps so they can label them, add voice recordings, or create a class book.

Using a Digital KWL Chart

Grade Level
1–3

Subject Area
Non-Fiction

iPad Comfort Level
Advanced

Suggested App
Padlet

Quick Tips
Visit innovatewithipad.com and click on Student Examples to find tips for creating QR codes.

Student Example
innovatewithipad.com

The Task
Before you begin teaching a new non-fiction topic, consider using a KWL chart (what I Know, what I Want to know, what I Learned) to find out what your students know and want to learn about the subject.

The Student's Learning Intention
- "I can use prior knowledge and schema to recall knowledge and ask questions for further inquiry."

The How
1. Go to Padlet.com and sign up for a free account.
2. Create three walls on Padlet:
   - "What I KNOW about _____."
   - "What I WANT to know about _____."
   - "What I LEARNED about_____."
3. Go to "Settings," then "Share."
4. Under the share option, there is a ready-made QR code.
5. Print the QR code for each Padlet wall.
6. Make a physical KWL chart and glue the appropriate QR code under each heading.
7. Have students come up to the chart, scan the QR code using the Padlet app under "K," and write what they know about your topic on the Padlet wall.
8. Have students repeat the process for "W."
9. Choose a non-fiction text about your topic to read aloud.
10. Have students scan the QR code for "L" and write about what they learned from the text.

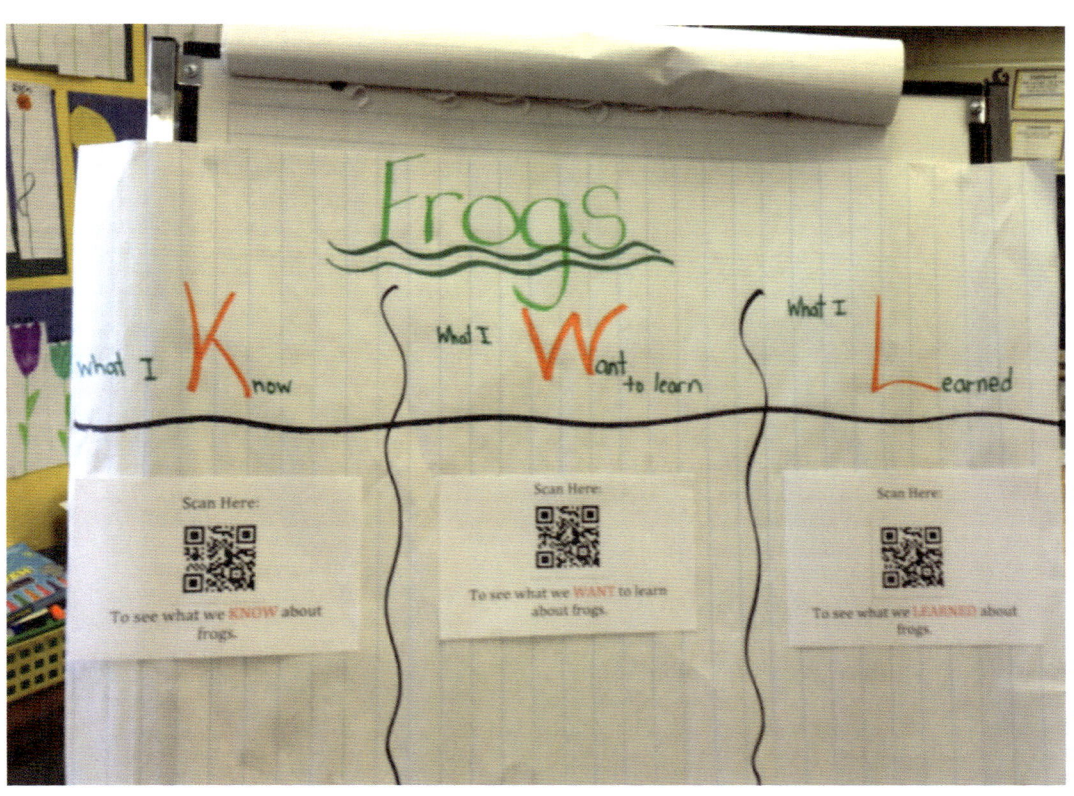

How to Create a Diagram in Book Creator

Grade Level

1–3

Subject Areas

Reading, Writing, Research Skills, Science

iPad Comfort Level

Beginner

Suggested App

Book Creator

Quick Tip

Encourage your students to find or draw an image with a white background so their diagram looks more professional.

Lesson Extension

Once students have finished their diagrams, have them add a new non-fiction text feature, like captions, to their book.

Task Card

innovatewithipad.com

The Task

Creating a digital non-fiction book at the end of an inquiry is a great way for students to show their learning. When modelling how to create a non-fiction book in Book Creator, make a Task Card for each feature you want your students to include. Students can either use a royalty-free image or draw a picture, making it easy to add their diagram's arrows and text.

The Student's Learning Intention

- "I create labelled diagrams to help my readers understand my text."

The How

1. Open Book Creator.
2. Tap New Book (top left).
3. Choose your template.
4. Tap the "+" (top right) to access everything you want to add to your page.
5. Using the text tool, add a title for your page (e.g., "Diagram of a _____") filling in the blank with your subject.
6. Tap "+" (top right) and then the image of a circle on top of a square next to Add Item.
7. Choose the arrow and place it where you want it to go.
8. Add your label.
9. Repeat this process until you have at least four labels.

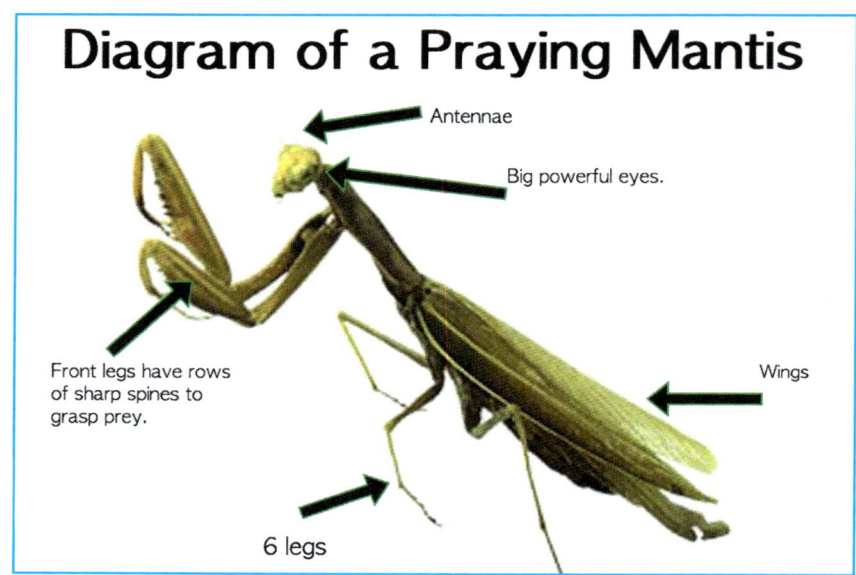

Creating a Non-Fiction Fact Web with Popplet

The Task

Popplet is a great tool to use when introducing students to the concept of jotting down notes while they research a project. If you have young learners, each popplet they create can become a page in their non-fiction book that they add to over the course of their research. Students love adding a picture of their topic in the middle of their popplet.

The Student's Learning Intentions

- "I gather information to support a non-fiction inquiry."
- "I determine whether or not facts are suitable for my purpose."

The How

1. Using a variety of sources, gather five interesting facts about an animal. Your sources can include read-alouds; mentor texts; shared, guided, and independent texts; videos; and media texts.
2. Open Popplet.
3. Touch your iPad's screen to create your first popple.
4. In the middle of the popple, add the name and a picture of the animal you are researching (the picture is optional).
5. Press one of the grey circles with a white circle inside of it to add another popple.
6. Type one fact you found during your research inside the popple.
7. Continue to create four more popples.
8. **When you are finished, tap Export to save and share your work.**

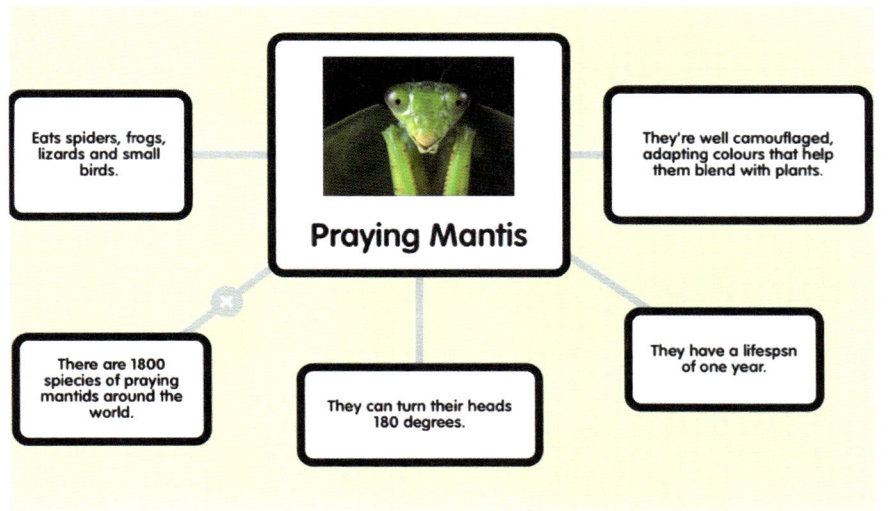

Eats spiders, frogs, lizards and small birds.	**Praying Mantis**	They're well camouflaged, adapting colours that help them blend with plants.
There are 1800 spiecies of praying mantids around the world.	They can turn their heads 180 degrees.	They have a lifespsn of one year.

Grade Level
1–3

Subject Area
Writing: Non-Fiction

iPad Comfort Level
Beginner

Suggested App
Popplet

chapter four

Science Lessons

Teacher-led inquiry and student-driven inquiry are among the most common practices you will find in today's science classroom, which is why we have designed many of the lessons in this chapter to focus on these processes. Like you, your students are sure to find these lessons meet their needs and are open-ended enough that they can easily show what they have learned.

Collecting Facts

Grade Level
1–3

Subject Area
Research Skills

iPad Comfort Level
Advanced

Suggested App
Popplet

Quick Tip
If students have a great deal of information in their popplet, they can easily see what they've added by expanding and shrinking the surface (pinching).

Lesson Extension
Have students add additional categories to sort information by, such as "Other Interesting Facts" which might include predators, or special, animal-specific adaptations.

The Task
This activity helps students organize information so they can more easily show their learning.

The Student's Learning Intention
- "I can sort information into can, have, and are."

The How
1. Select your primary sources for information gathering. These can be books, websites, or apps.
2. Open Popplet.
3. Add a title that tells the reader what you are studying.
4. Create three popples across the top of the page.
5. Assign each popple a heading: "Can," "Have," and "Are."
6. Review your primary sources. Create a popple for each fact you have collected.
7. Place each popple under its proper heading.
8. Continue reviewing your information and creating popples until all of your facts are in the popplet.
9. Save your popplet to the Camera Roll.

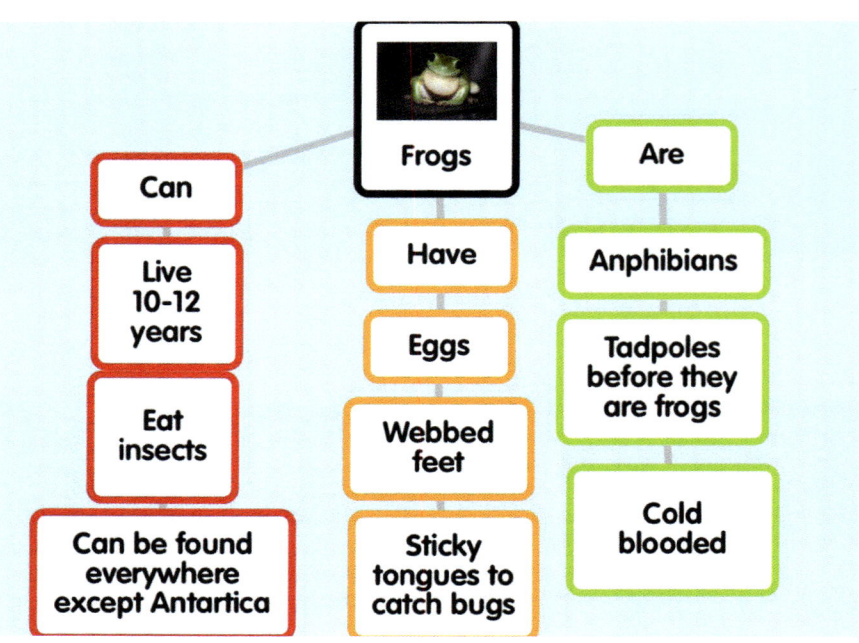

The Parts of a Plant

The Task

It's important for students to be able to recognize and label a plant's parts.

The Student's Learning Intention

- "I can label the parts of a plant."

The How

1. Take a photo of your plant with your iPad.
2. Open Explain Everything.
3. Import your image or capture a photo with the app.
4. Label the plant's parts in the photo using the arrow and text tools.
5. When you are pleased with how you have annotated your image, save or share your labelled image by tapping the box with the arrow coming out of it (top right).

Grade Level
1

Subject Area
Plants

iPad Comfort Level
Beginner

Suggested App
Explain Everything

Lesson Extension
Students can record their voices explaining each plant part's function.

Signs of the Season

Grade Level
K–1

Subject Area
Seasons

iPad Comfort Level
Beginner

Suggested App
Popplet/Popplet Lite

Lesson Extensions

During the course of the school year, have students make a popplet for each season. At the end of the year, create a book featuring all four seasons.

Have students import their images into an app with a voice-recording feature so they can explain why they chose their images.

The Task

In this open problem, students use Popplet and their iPad's camera to capture and document a season using visual signs.

The Student's Learning Intention

- "I can identify a season's signs."

The How

1. Go on a walk in the schoolyard.
2. Using your iPad's camera, capture signs of the current season. For example, in the fall you might take a picture of the leaves changing colours.
3. Once you have taken your photos, open Popplet.
4. Touch the screen to create your popplet's first popple.
5. Use the text feature and write your popplet's title. For example, "Signs of Winter."
6. Add more popples, each containing an image of a sign of the season.
7. Continue to create popples as needed.
8. When you are finished, tap Export to save or share your popplet.

Signs of Spring

Solids, Liquids, and Gases

Grade Level
2–3

Subject Area
States of Matter

iPad Comfort Level
Beginner

Suggested App
Pic Collage

The Task

After investigating the properties of solids, liquids, and gases, your students can engage in this great culminating activity by taking pictures in the classroom of the states of matter and correctly labelling them.

The Student's Learning Intentions

- "I know there are three states of matter: solid, liquid, and gas."
- "I can take or find pictures of each form of matter."

The How

1. Use your iPad to take pictures of at least six different objects that you can identify as a solid, liquid, or gas.
2. Open Pic Collage.
3. Tap "+" to start a new collage.
4. Press the "+" (bottom) and select up to twelve photos from your Camera Roll to add to your collage.
5. Tap the checkmark (top right corner of each photo).
6. At this point, you can either organize your images freehand or tap the grid square (bottom left) to select the grid that best fits your images.
7. Tap the "+" button again to add text.
8. Label your pictures as a solid, liquid, or gas. Once you have finished, add your name.
9. Tap the box with the arrow pointing out from it to save your collage to your iPad's Camera Roll. To share your collage on social media, in an email, or to your Google Drive, select the appropriate option.

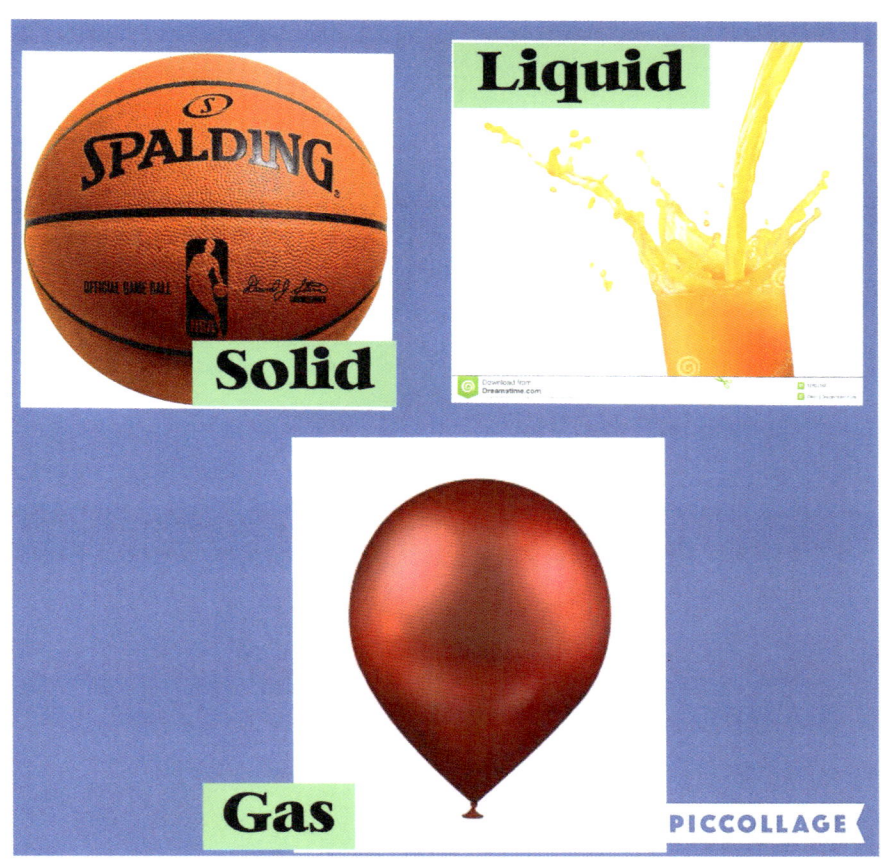

The Water Cycle with Pic Collage

Grade Level
2–3

Subject Area
Water Cycle

iPad Comfort Level
Advanced

Suggested App
Pic Collage

Quick Tip
Animated GIFs are exciting to look at. Unfortunately, when students save their collages to their iPad's Camera Roll, the GIFs' movements don't work.

Lesson Extension
Have students use a drawing app to draw each stage of the water cycle and then add their drawings to the collage.

The Task
Your students will create a picture collage that shows their understanding of the water cycle.

The Student's Learning Intention
- "I can create the water cycle."

The How
1. Open Pic Collage.
2. Tap "+" to start a new collage.
3. Push the "+" (bottom) and select Web Search from within the app.
4. In the search bar within the app, type the water cycle's features.
5. From the app search, select the image that best represents each part of the water cycle and add it to the collage.
6. Continue the process until every feature is represented. Arrange your images to reflect the order of the water cycle.
7. Tap "+" (bottom) and select the text tool to label to your collage.
8. Push the "+" and select the sticker feature.
9. Choose the arrow sticker and add arrows where needed.
10. When you have finished labelling your project, add your name.
11. Press the box with the arrow pointing out from it to save your collage to the Camera Roll. To share your collage on social media, via email, or to your Google Drive, select the appropriate option.

The Water Cycle

Condensation

Evaporation,

Precipitation

PicCOLLAGE

The Water Cycle with Explain Everything

Grade Level
2–3

Subject Area
Water Cycle

iPad Comfort Level
Beginner

Suggested Apps
Popplet
Explain Everything
Drawing Pad
BrainPOP Jr. Movie
  of the Week

Quick Tip
If BrainPOP Jr. is not an option for you, having students read through a basket of books or watch a YouTube video about the water cycle would work well, too.

Task Card
innovatewithipad.com

The Task
BrainPOP Jr. is an amazing website geared towards K-3 students with an extensive library of short, five-minute videos about every subject's key curriculum topics. Use your projector to show BrainPOP Jr. videos so the entire class can watch together, or download the BrainPOP Jr. Movie of the Week app to your students' iPads so they can watch independently or with a partner.

The Student's Learning Intentions
- "I can investigate and explain the water cycle."
- "I use the appropriate vocabulary in my explanation."

The How
1. Open the BrainPOP Jr. Movie of the Week app.
2. Choose the Water Cycle movie.
3. As you watch the video, think about the following questions:
   - What is the water cycle?
   - What happens when water heats up?
   - What happens to water vapour in the atmosphere?
   - What is precipitation?
   - How can we care for our water?
4. Create an artifact on your iPad to show your learning. You may want to use Popplet, Explain Everything, or Drawing Pad.

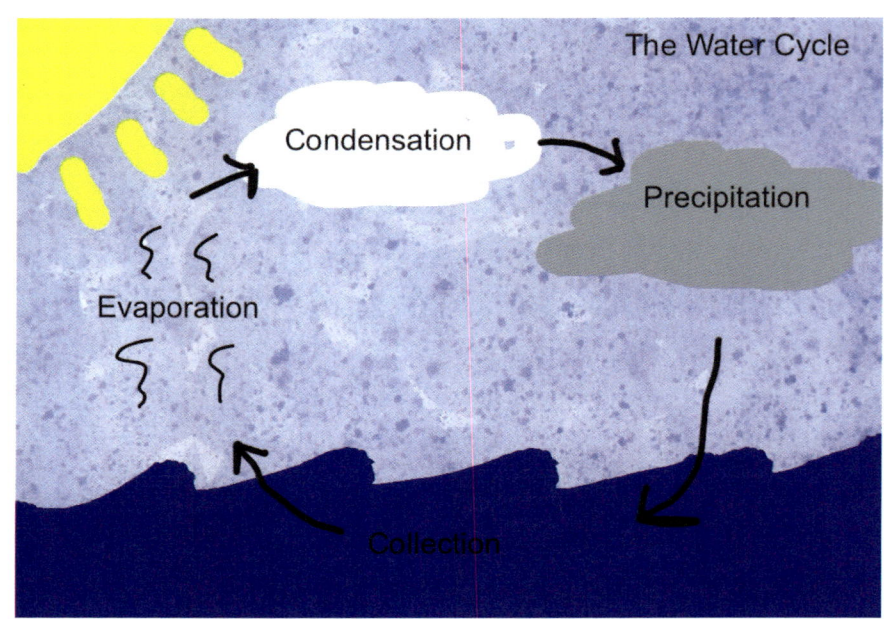

Living and Non-Living Things

The Task

It's important for students to understand that objects are either living or non-living. In this activity, students draw or capture important objects and then classify them as living or non-living, an activity so simple that even your youngest learners can grasp the concept.

The Student's Learning Intention

- "I categorize objects as living or non-living."

The How

1. Go for a walk outside and take photos of living and non-living objects.
2. Return to the classroom and review your photos, determining which images are of living things and which ones are of non-living things.
3. Open Book Creator.
4. Tap New Book (top left).
5. Choose your template and give your book a title.
6. Tap the "+" button (top right) to access your photos.
7. On each page, add a photo of something living or non-living. If you prefer, use the drawing tools and draw a picture in Book Creator or import drawings you created in another app.
8. For each image, record yourself explaining if the object is living or non-living and how you know (if you can).
9. If you are able, label each object as living or non-living.
10. Save your finished project to your Camera Roll.

Grade Level
K–1

Subject Area
Living and Non-Living

iPad Comfort Level
Beginner

Suggested App
Book Creator

Student Example
innovatewithipad.com

Recreating an Animal's Life Cycle

Grade Level
1–3

Subject Area
Animal Life Cycle

iPad Comfort Level
Advanced

Suggested App
Popplet/Popplet Lite

Quick Tip
Use this app in landscape for a larger work area.

Lesson Extension
Ask your students to demonstrate how a frog's life cycle differs from other animals'.

Task Card
innovatewithipad.com

The Task
In this lesson, students learn about a frog's growth cycle. Your students will either draw or find pictures, and then label their images to show their thinking and knowledge.

The Student's Learning Intentions
- "I can describe each stage in a frog's life cycle."
- "I can identify the stages of the life cycle of the frog using the correct vocabulary."

The How
1. Open Popplet.
2. Tap the screen to create your first popple.
3. Use the text feature (bottom) and write your popplet's title: "The Life Cycle of a Frog."
4. Add more popples, each containing an image of a life cycle stage.
5. When you are finished, tap Export to save or share your popplet.

The Five Senses

The Task

This lesson introduces students to their five senses through observation and exploration. Students learn the vocabulary of sight, hearing, taste, touch, and smell, and relate each sense to its corresponding sensory organ.

The Student's Learning Intentions

- "I can name the five senses and the body part used for each."
- "I can verbally match pictures of body parts to the sense that goes with them."

The How

1. Open your iPad's camera app and take pictures of the five body parts that represent the five senses.
2. Open Explain Everything.
3. Tap the "+" button to select a colour template.
4. Tap "+" again and select Photo, Video, or File.
5. Choose Photo.
6. Select the Camera Roll.
7. Select and insert your five senses pictures. You may create five separate slides, one for each sense, or one slide and put all of the pictures on it.
8. Press the record button and explain the body's five senses, being sure to name each sense's corresponding body part.
9. Save your video to the Camera Roll.

Grade Level
1

Subject Area
Five Senses

iPad Comfort Level
Beginner

Suggested Apps
Explain Everything
Pic Collage
Popplet

Quick Tip

When they record their thinking, encourage students to point at the image they're explaining using Explain Everything's laser pointer.

Pumpkin Inquiry

Grade Level
K–3

Subject Area
Inquiry

iPad Comfort Level
Beginner

Suggested App
Book Creator

Quick Tip
Remind your students that their iPad's microphone is highly sensitive, so they need to speak clearly when recording themselves. Do an in-class demonstration, and show students how rubbing your fingers over the microphone while it's recording makes a very loud sound.

Student Example
innovatewithipad.com

The Task
Pumpkins are fascinating fruits, and there's no better way to learn more about them than through the inquiry process. This activity blends hands-on exploration with digital documentation to help students create a pumpkin resource book.

The Student's Learning Intentions
- "I can make predictions based on my background knowledge."
- "I can estimate how many seeds a pumpkin has."
- "I can count the number of seeds a pumpkin has."
- "I can explore a pumpkin's properties."

The How
1. Look at the four pumpkins in your classroom.
2. Take a photo of each pumpkin.
3. Make a prediction about how many seeds you think are in each pumpkin.
4. Open Book Creator.
5. Create a new book.
6. Tap the "+" button (top right) to access your photos.
7. Add your pictures of the pumpkins.
8. Write or record your seed predictions.
9. Document your predictions in your book.
10. Your teacher will measure a string that goes around each pumpkin while you are documenting your predictions in your book.
11. Take a photo of each string and decide which pumpkin the string fits around. Record your prediction using your voice or keypad.
12. Match the strings to the pumpkins and record these results using images, your voice, or text.
13. In a group, select one of the pumpkins to open and scoop out your seeds.
14. Sort the seeds into piles of ten.
15. Take photos of your piles and count your seeds.
16. Record how many seeds you have in your book.
17. Collect information from your classmates about their seeds.
18. Add your classmates' information to your book.
19. Create additional pages to share what you have learned about pumpkins and what questions you still have.
20. Save your finished book to the Camera Roll.

Lesson Extensions

Have students predict how much their pumpkins weigh, and then weigh the pumpkins.

Change up the lesson, and use different-coloured pumpkins. Prompt students to make predictions about each pumpkin's weight based on its colour.

If your students have additional questions, create activities centred on helping them find answers, being sure to record their findings in their books.

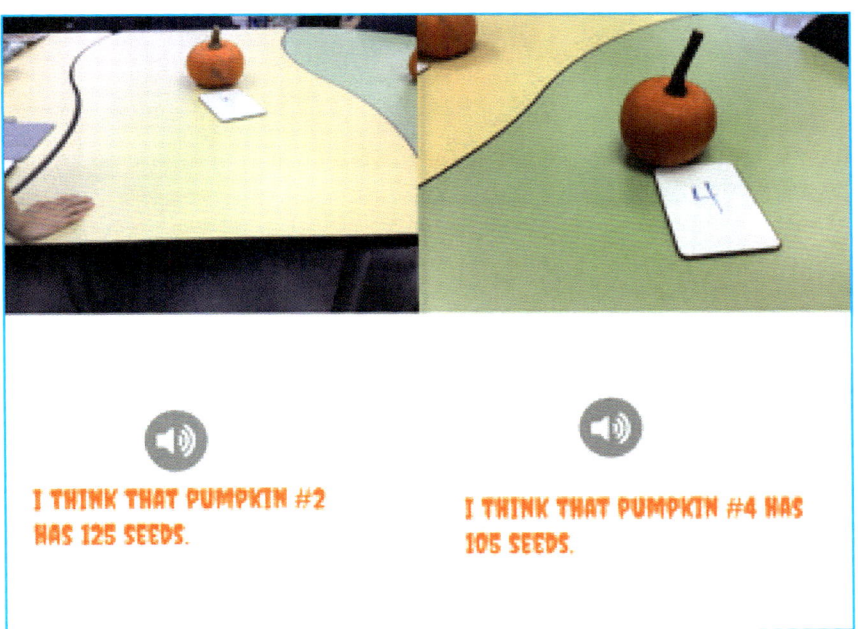

I THINK THAT PUMPKIN #2 HAS 125 SEEDS.

I THINK THAT PUMPKIN #4 HAS 105 SEEDS.

Created by Sajjad S. Surrey, BC, Canada

Push and Pull Forces

Grade Level
1

Subject Area
Force and Motion

iPad Comfort Level
Beginner

Suggested App
Popplet

Quick Tips
Before they search for images on Pixabay.com, either individually or as a class, students should brainstorm ideas for objects or activities that illustrate pushing and pulling.

Demonstrate how to download images from Pixabay (by touching the image to reveal the Save Image option).

Lesson Extension
Challenge your students to think of activities that require both push and pull forces, such as skipping.

The Task
This activity encourages students to think about places where push and pull forces are applied.

The Student's Learning Intention
- "I can identify actions that demonstrate the push and pull forces."

The How
1. Either take photos of push and pull examples in your environment or go to Pixabay.com, search for, and save images to your Camera Roll. Pixabay is a free-use website, and its images do not require citations.
2. Open Popplet.
3. Title your popplet "Push and Pull."
4. Create a popple and title it "Push."
5. Add your images showing push.
6. Create a new popple and title it "Pull."
7. Add your pull images.
8. **Save the popplet to your iPad's Camera Roll.**

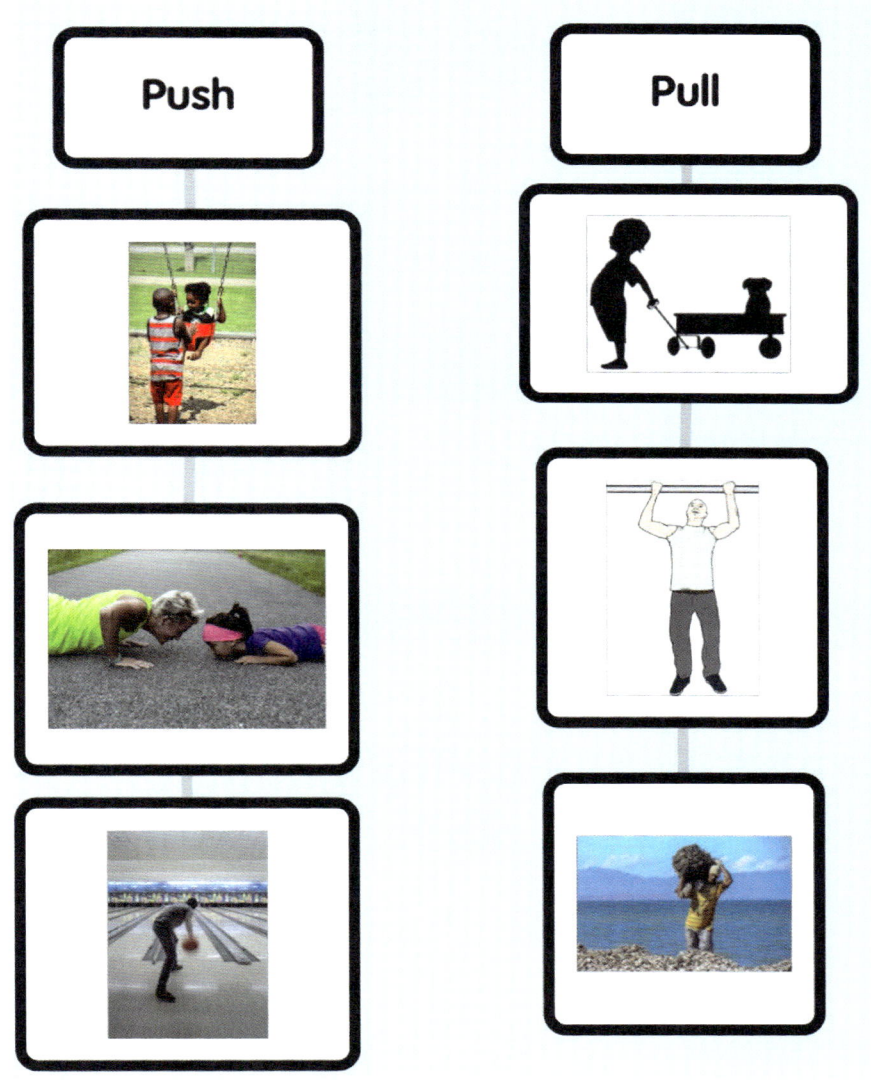

| Push | Pull |

chapter five

Social Studies Lessons

One of the best things about using iPads in your classroom is that each student can document their learning in the way that works best for them. In this chapter, we explore a few key lessons to show you how your classroom's iPads can support a social studies curriculum. And since social studies content can vary greatly from school district to school district, feel free to adapt and modify our lessons to fit your teaching environment.

Getting to Know Me

Grade Level

K–3

Subject Area

All about Me

iPad Comfort Level

Beginner

Suggested App

Pic Collage

Quick Tip

Though students can download animated GIF images from the Internet, Pic Collage won't save an animated GIF's movement to the Camera Roll.

Lesson Extension

Use the sticker options to add more details to your collage and the text tool to label your images.

The Task

As you start a new school year, it's a great idea to take some time and get to know your students. Pic Collage helps students make a personal collage to share with you what they are passionate about.

The Student's Learning Intention

- "I can create a collage that reflects what is important to me."

The How

1. Open Pic Collage.
2. Create a new collage.
3. Tap the "+" button (bottom).
4. If you have images already on your device, select those photos and upload them to your collage. However, if you do not have images, select Web Search from within the app, search for things important to you, and then upload them to your collage. When images are searched from within the app, they are cited appropriately. Either way, you may choose up to twelve images.
5. Place your images around the collage.
6. Select your background.
7. Give your collage a title such as "All About Me."
8. Save to your collage to the Camera Roll.

Ways to Help the World

Grade Level
1

Subject Area
Our World

iPad Comfort Level
Beginner

Suggested App
Popplet

Quick Tips

Encourage your students to brainstorm their ideas for ways they can help the global community before they start searching for images on Pixabay.com.

Demonstrate how to download images from Pixabay.

Discourage your students from doing a general Internet search for images.

Note: since Pixabay is a free-use website, images don't require citations.

Lesson Extension

Challenge your students to think of ways they can contribute positively to their school, community, city, and beyond. Have them create a popplet featuring their ideas for helping in each environment.

The Task

It is important for students to look beyond themselves and think of others. Popplet is an excellent tool to use to help a student document their thinking and actions.

The Student's Learning Intention

- "I can identify actions that help the world."

The How

1. Brainstorm ways you can help others.
2. Go to Pixabay.com. Search for and save free-use images that support your brainstorming.
3. Open Popplet.
4. Create a popple.
5. Upload your first image and add text explaining how the action in the image helps the world.
6. Repeat the process until all of your images are in popples.
7. Give your popplet a title.
8. Save your popplet to your iPad's Camera Roll.

Created by Sajjad S. and Jesse S, Surrey, BC, Canada

Healthy or Not Healthy?

Grade Level
K–3

Subject Area
Personal Health

iPad Comfort Level
Beginner

Suggested App
Pic Collage

Quick Tip
If your students receive a hot lunch at school, have them find images on Pixabay.com using Pic Collage's image search feature.

Lesson Extension
If you have older students, encourage them to sort their lunch into the food groups.

Task Card
innovatewithipad.com

The Task
This is a fun activity to do when you're teaching students how to make healthy eating choices. To model this activity, take out your own lunch, photograph each item with your iPad, and then use Pic Collage to categorize each food as either "Healthy" or "Not Healthy."

The Student's Learning Intention
- "I demonstrate an understanding of factors that contribute to healthy food choices."

The How
1. Take out the foods in your lunch.
2. Using your iPad's camera, take a photo of each item.
3. Open Pic Collage.
4. Start a new collage and press the "+" button.
5. Touch the pink text button.
6. Type "Healthy" and then tap the checkmark.
7. Press the pink text button again.
8. Type "Not Healthy."
9. Place your labels at the top of your collage, side by side.
10. Press "+" and choose the green photos option.
11. Select the photos of your lunch and tap each picture's checkmark.
12. Categorize each food as either "Healthy" or "Not Healthy."
13. Save your work to your iPad's Camera Roll.

Communities

Grade Level
K–3

Subject Area
Community

iPad Comfort Level
Beginner

Suggested App
Popplet/Popplet Lite

Quick Tip
If you don't have Popplet on your iPad, you could also use Pic Collage.

Lesson Extension
Students could use Google Earth to check out communities near or far away from them and then compare those communities to theirs in a Venn diagram.

Task Card
innovatewithipad.com

The Task
By focusing on urban and rural communities' differences and similarities, students become more aware of how the region they live in compares to others nearby and far away.

The Student's Learning Intentions
- "I identify distinguishing features of urban and rural communities."
- "I describe possible relationships between communities and natural environments."
- "I demonstrate an awareness of the possible differences and similarities among environments."
- "I demonstrate an understanding of urban and rural communities' characteristics."

The How
1. Open Popplet.
2. Touch the screen to create a popple.
3. Use the text feature and write the title of your popplet. For example, your title could be "Communities."
4. Create two popples, labelling them "Urban" and "Rural."
5. Add more popples, each containing an image, text, or picture representing an urban or rural community's characteristic.
6. When you have finished, tap Export to save or share your popplet.

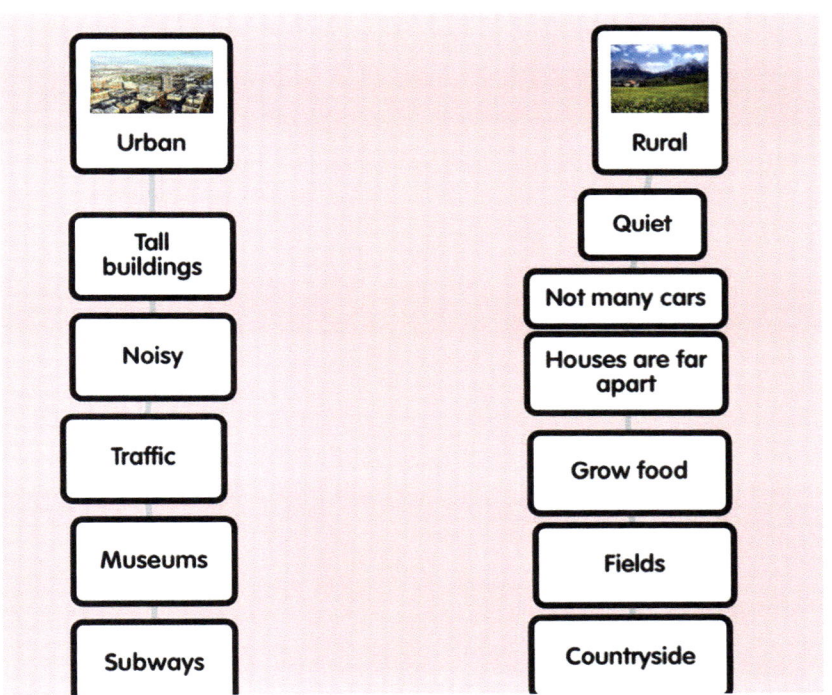

Urban	Rural
Tall buildings	Quiet
Noisy	Not many cars
Traffic	Houses are far apart
Museums	Grow food
Subways	Fields
	Countryside

Being Healthy

Grade Level
K–3

Subject Area
Personal Health

iPad Comfort Level
Beginner

Suggested Apps
Drawing Pad
Doodle Buddy
Drawing App of
  Your Choice

Lesson Extensions
Encourage your students to better explain their thinking by either importing their drawings into an app with a voice-recording feature or by adding text.

Ask students to create more than one image and then combine their images in iMovie, Book Creator, or Explain Everything to make a movie or book about healthy habits.

The Task
Many young learners tend to show their learning better through images than in words. So, using their iPads' drawing tools, your students can share their knowledge of the healthy habits they are developing.

The Student's Learning Intention
• "I can show habits that support a healthy lifestyle."

The How
1. Open your favourite drawing app.
2. Think about what you know about a healthy lifestyle's habits.
3. Divide your paper (screen) into four sections.
4. In each section, draw a healthy habit.
5. Save your drawing to the Camera Roll.

chapter six

Self-Assessment

Self-assessments are key to students' continued improvement. With their iPad's help, students can easily set and track goals, assess their learning, and reflect on lessons. This chapter provides several simple, but powerful, ways for even your youngest learners to use the iPad in a self-assessment.

Let Your Thinking Be Heard

Grade Level
K–3

Subject Area
All Content Areas

iPad Comfort Level
Advanced

Suggested Apps
Draw and Tell
Book Creator
Explain Everything
Doodlecast Pro
30hands
Shadow Puppet Edu

Lesson Extensions
Don't limit voice recordings to simply sharing thinking; rather, have students record what they are proud of and what they'd like to work on.

Take this lesson a step further, and have your students record their assessment of a friend's project so their friend can improve as well.

The Task
Ever wondered what your students were thinking when they created a project? Now they can explain their thoughts in their own voice and using their own words with the help of their iPad. Students can use any iPad voice-recording app that allows them to import an image.

The Student's Learning Intention
• "I can record my voice explaining my thinking about _____."

The How
1. If you would like to reflect on non-digital work, capture an image of it; however, if you created your work on an iPad, take a screenshot and save it to the Camera Roll.
2. Open Draw and Tell.
3. Select and import your image from the Camera Roll. (In Draw and Tell, you can access the Camera Roll import option by tapping the image of the paper with two children.)
4. Press the record button and then record yourself explaining your thinking.
5. Once you have finished, tap the left arrow (top left).
6. Save your creation to the Camera Roll.

Checking My Reading Fluency

The Task

When teaching your class about reading fluency, having students hear themselves read is very important. In this activity, students record themselves reading a "just right book," and then choose a goal to work on for the next reading.

The Student's Learning Intention

- "I read accurately and fluently to support my comprehension."

The How

1. Choose a book from the class's book bin.
2. Open Explain Everything.
3. Take a picture of the text you'll be reading.
4. Press the red button to record your voice.
5. Read your book for one minute (a timer is at the bottom of the screen).
6. Press the play button to listen to yourself reading.
7. Fill out the Fluency Evaluation sheet and choose a goal for your next reading.
8. Slide the recording strip back to the beginning and re-record yourself reading the same text, concentrating on your goal.
9. Play your second recording. Did you improve?
10. Save your recording to your iPad, using your name and the date in the file name.

Grade Level
1–3

Subject Area
Reading Fluency

iPad Comfort Level
Beginner

Suggested App
Explain Everything

Quick Tip

Rather than taking a picture of the book, using Explain Everything's video option, students can prop up their iPad, place their book in the shot, and record themselves reading.

Self-Assessment of Criteria

Grade Level
K–3

Subject Area
All Areas

iPad Comfort Level
Advanced

Suggested App
Explain Everything

Quick Tip
To change the pencil tool's colour from solid to translucent, tap the colour box and slide the opacity slider. If you can't see the slider, draw a line under the criterion and its corresponding proof instead of highlighting it.

Lesson Extension
Prompt students to add a self-reflection recording to the image.

The Task

In this activity, students will self-assess in order to prove they have met criteria through annotation.

The Student's Learning Intention

- "I can identify where I have met criteria for success."

The How

1. Take a photo of the document with the criteria needed to meet the lesson's objective.
2. Photograph your finished product (or take a screenshot if your project is digital).
3. Open Explain Everything and start a new project.
4. Import the photos of your criteria and completed work.
5. Using the pencil tool, highlight the first criterion.
6. Highlight the proof that you have met that criterion in the same colour.
7. Repeat the process for all of the criteria, choosing different colours for each.
8. Save your work to the Camera Roll.

I can explain why he should or should not squish him. I can give at least two reasons.

What does good writing look like.

1. Doing your own work.
2. Use periods, full stops, question marks.
3. Try your best.
4. Use capital letters where needed.
5. Use your word wall word.

Hey Little Ant
What do you think the boy should do?

I think he shouldnt
be squished because he
is part of nater. If
I was an ant I wodint
want to be squished. all
becace I love insecs.

Created by Mya L. Surrey, BC, Canada

A Self-Reflecting Writer

Grade Level
K–3

Subject Area
Writing

iPad Comfort Level
Advanced

Suggested Apps
Draw and Tell
Explain Everything
30hands
Shadow Puppet Edu
Doodlecast

Quick Tip
In Draw and Tell, you can only record once, meaning you must start over if you make a mistake. Book Creator and iMovie, however, allow you to record your thinking more than once on the same page.

Lesson Extension
Have students take a photo of two of their writing samples side by side, and then record themselves talking about the improvements they notice.

The Task
In this simple activity, young learners read, reflect on, and set goals for their writing. Students also take an active role in their learning and express what they are proud of, as well as what they still need to work on (and how they will do it).

The Student's Learning Intentions
- "I reflect on my writing by sharing the areas I have been working on."
- "I reflect on my writing by sharing what I'd like to continue to improve."
- "I set goals to improve my writing."
- "I suggest ways to support my writing."

The How
1. Either take a photo of your non-digital writing sample or a screenshot of a digital sample.
2. Open Draw and Tell.
3. Make your writing sample image the background image. (Tap the paper option that has an image with two children to access Draw and Tell's Camera Roll option.)
4. Tap the microphone button to activate your iPad's mic.
5. Record yourself reading your writing sample.
6. End your reading with self-reflection, sharing what you have been working on in your writing and which areas you would like to continue improving. Set a new writing goal.
7. Once you have finished, tap the left arrow (top left).
8. Save your creation to the iPad's Camera Roll.

Acknowledgments

Karen Lirenman

I would like to thank Tia Henriksen, my friend and administrator who gently encouraged me to join Twitter back in the summer of 2011. Without her nudging, I never would have met my #1stchat and #ADE friends, who make up the incredible personal learning network that continually challenges and inspires me to be a better educator.

I would also like to acknowledge Elisa Carlson, Surrey Schools' former director of instruction. She had a vision for innovative change, and believed in and championed my work from the very beginning. She allowed me to take risks and discover new and better ways to support my students and their learning. This book never would have happened without her incredible support.

Thank you students Jaslehna G., Mya L., Sajjad S., and Jesse S. and their parents for allowing us to include images of their work in this book.

Finally, I want to thank my parents, David and the late Terry Lirenman, for fostering my curiosity and raising me to be a life-long learner. They always told me to be sure to do what makes me happy.

Kristen Wideen

I would first like to thank my husband, Eric Wideen, who has been a constant source of support and encouragement since the day we met. Thank you for being an amazing father and friend, and for keeping our crazy life balanced. Your love, support, and partnership mean more to me than you will ever know.

I would also like to thank James Cowper, the administrator who pushed me to rethink my role as an educator. Without your leadership and support, I would not have had the confidence to take the risks that have led to this amazing journey. (Who would have ever thought that asking for a single iPad could have transformed my thinking on so many levels?) Thank you for encouraging me to take chances, persevere, and always look forward.

Finally, I would like to thank my personal cheerleaders, my parents, Carol and Rick Reddam. No matter what I do or where this life takes me, I know they will always be in the front row, cheering me on.

About the Authors

Karen Lirenman is an award-winning primary school teacher who is transforming education by connecting her students with the world through Twitter, blogs, and video conferencing. She takes a hands-on approach to teaching by including inquiry, projects, and the maker mindset in her classroom. Her students choose how they learn, show, and share their knowledge.

Karen earned her bachelor of arts degree, bachelor of education degree, and a diploma in Teaching English as a Second Language from the University of British Columbia. She has taught in both Australia and Canada. Karen is an Apple Distinguished Educator and a Google for Education Certified Innovator. She blogs regularly at www.klirenman.com.

Kristen Wideen has spent her career teaching and engaging primary school children in the United States and Canada. Through her innovative, student-driven projects, she teaches classes to take chances and develop the skills necessary to succeed in the twenty-first century. Kristen encourages her students to create, collaborate, and be open to try new things in her classroom every day.

She earned her bachelor's degree in education through the University of Windsor, completed her master's in the art of teaching at Marygrove College in Detroit, Michigan, and is recognized as an Apple Distinguished Educator. She frequently writes about her educational journey at MrsWideen.com, and enjoys inspiring educators to use technology in innovative ways by speaking at conferences.

Printed in Great Britain
by Amazon